ELEGANT

26 Projects for Creating Your Own Luxurious Linens

LINENS

CHIPPY IRVINE

Special Photography by Alex McLean

A BULFINCH PRESS BOOK

LITTLE, BROWN AND COMPANY

BOSTON   NEW YORK   TORONTO   LONDON

FIRST EDITION

Library of Congress Cataloging-in-Publication Data
Irvine, Chippy.
Elegant linens : 26 projects for creating your own
luxurious linens / by Chippy Irvine. — 1st ed.
p. cm.
"A Bulfinch Press book."
Includes bibliographical references.
ISBN 0-8212-2380-1
1. Household linens. 2. Needlework. I. Title.
TT387.I78   1998
746.9'6 — dc21   97-43444

Bulfinch Press is an imprint and trademark of
Little, Brown and Company (Inc.)
Published simultaneously in Canada by
Little, Brown & Company (Canada) Limited

PRINTED IN SINGAPORE

In memory of my great-aunts
Polly and Lizzie,
who died before I was born
but whose embroidery on household linens
inspired me to write this book

CONTENTS
with List of Projects

INTRODUCTION   I

CHAPTER ONE ❋ MATERIALS: FABRICS,
TRIMMINGS, AND EMBROIDERY   II

CHAPTER TWO ❋ SEWING EQUIPMENT
AND TECHNIQUES   25

    Flat Pincushion   29

CHAPTER THREE ❋ FRONT ROOMS: DINING
ROOMS, LIVING ROOMS, AND STUDIES   37

    Winter Napkins and Napkin Rings   43
    Summer Napkins and Napkin Rings   44
    Place Mats with Double Welt   46
    Table Runner   50
    Cocktail Napkins   52
    Square Tablecloth   56
    Lined Circular Table Skirt   56
    Unlined Square Tablecloth with Border 58
    Matching Quilted Circular Table Skirt 59
    Mitered Striped Table Skirt   60

CHAPTER FOUR ❋ WORK ROOMS:
KITCHENS, PANTRIES, AND LAUNDRIES   62

    Baby's Bib   68
    Tea Cozy   70
    Laundry Caddy   74

Contents

CHAPTER FIVE ✷ UPSTAIRS: BEDROOMS,
DRESSING ROOMS, AND BATHROOMS   76

Quilted Tuck-in Bedspread   82
Simple Lace Curtains   88
Multiple Shoe Holder   90
Under-Sink Curtain   96
Simple Bathrobe   98

CHAPTER SIX ✷ OUTSIDE: PATIOS,
POOL HOUSES, AND GARDENS   100

Mitered Striped Pillow Covers   104
Seat Pad for a Porch Rocking Chair   106
Gardening Apron   110
Kneeling Pad   112
*Lined Picnic Hamper with Cloth
and Napkins*   113

CHAPTER SEVEN ✷ CARE, REPAIR,
AND STORAGE OF LINENS   115

Sewing Sheets Sides to Middle   123
Striped Taffeta Sachet   126

BASIC AND USEFUL STITCHES   128
GLOSSARY   133
SOURCES   144
SELECTED BIBLIOGRAPHY   151

 HAVE ALWAYS been fascinated by some linens made by two great-aunts of mine who died before I was born. On the top landing of our house, outside the nursery bedroom, was a chest of drawers full of real linen sheets, lace-trimmed pillow slips, white damask tablecloths stiff with starch, embroidered tray cloths, tatted doilies, and crochet-edged guest towels, all handmade by Aunt Polly and Aunt Lizzie, my grandmother's sisters. The accumulation had been started for their "bottom drawers," or hope chests.

Neither of my great-aunts married, but they became famous locally as talented and unstoppable seamstresses. My mother, their niece, inherited this profusion of stitchery, which included a complete wardrobe of clothes for her jointed china doll.

My mother seldom used the beautiful, elaborately decorated pillow slips, towels, and tablecloths because they were "a bother." She was a musician, a singer, and a teacher — not a traditional housewife — and almost never sewed. Sewing, to her, was such a chore she stashed mending in an upholstered box stool that she called the "sit-and-think-it-over" and would finally attack it only as a Lenten penance.

OPPOSITE: *An early-eighteenth-century English cabinet designed by architect William Kent holds table linens.*

PREVIOUS PAGES:
LEFT: *A tiny circle of cotton damask — no doubt recycled from an old tablecloth — is surrounded by a wide band of tatting. This doily, made circa 1880, sits on an eighteenth-century candle stand.*
RIGHT: *A deep closet at the end of a hallway holds quilts, pillows, coverlets, seat pads, curtains, and a small rattan stool to enable one to reach the higher shelves.*

I get great pleasure from unfolding and cherishing beautiful hand-embroidered vintage or heirloom linens. They are a reminder that young girls in the past became expert seamstresses, sewing enough household linen to fill their dowry chests, and every minute stitch had to be worked by hand. Before television, there was time and skill to spare as women and children — and in some cases men — turned their talents to refined creativity. Now we marvel at the sewing methods of these adept brides, artistic mothers, and maiden aunts and can be inspired by their patterns for embroidery and lace.

In the seventeenth and eighteenth centuries, before the great influx of American cotton to Europe, bed sheets — for those wealthy enough to have them — were made of linen, or, for the less well heeled, of hemp, which was coarser. When traveling in style, ladies and gentlemen often brought their own sheets, together with plates and eating implements. Now we use the term *household linen* (or *domestic linen*) loosely to include fabric items made of many fibers besides linen. Real linen sheets and embroidered linen pillowcases have become luxury items because they take time and skill to wash and iron. The bonus is that pure linen looks and feels wonderful when correctly laundered. Cotton linens come in many qualities and "counts" (the number of threads per inch) and are more to contemporary taste, though pure cotton often needs careful ironing to look its best. And these days, of course, there are many different blends of cotton and polyester, which helps to lessen laundry chores.

Traditionally, the linen closet also held the trousseau — handmade lingerie that would see the bride through many years. In an article written in the 1930s about preparations for a wedding, Nancy

Towels can be stored on open shelves in a bathroom.

OPPOSITE: *Cherished items in a linen closet might include a christening robe and petticoat such as these, made in 1889, that have been used in our family for three generations.*

Mitford wrote: "The heroine is now free to give her whole mind to her trousseau. 'All I want in the way of undies,' she explains to the confidante, who is naturally all attention, 'is a dozen sets of pink satin, which is much more chic now than crêpe de Chine, don't you think? and about a dozen pairs of pajamas. With a few slips to wear under cotton frocks, that is really enough, and by having little I can afford to have real lace on everything.'"

"Real" lace was important in my mother's day. By that, of course, was meant handmade lace, which was then still to be found in other than antique shops. Even Mother, who thought most fine linens were a bother, would point out that all the tiny, pleasing imperfections made handmade lace much more desirable than the impersonal exactness of machine-made lace. Mr. Cochran, of revue fame, demanded that his famously stylish chorus girls have "real Val lace" on their under-petticoats because then they would comport themselves like ladies.

The handmade touch *is* important — the one-of-a-kind patchwork quilt, the hand-crocheted bedspread, the hand-embroidered Belgian wedding handkerchief, custom-made lingerie, the specially commissioned linen tablecloth from Ireland. As I examine heirloom linens, I search for tactile information about the stitcher: What was she, or he, like? There are clues in the way they solved their craft problems, in the well-concealed knots of thread on the back, in the closely packed embroidered stitches on the front. There is history, especially in embroidery from before this century, when commercial embroidery patterns were rare and the designs were therefore unique. There is history too in handmade lace, from sixteenth-century ruffs onward, which made various countries and towns famous for their individual lace styles. (For those who want to pursue the remarkable history of lace, the best book around is *Lace: A History*, by Santine M. Levey, listed in the bibliography of this book.)

The linen closet might also include a layette for the hoped-for baby. Piles of tiny lace-edged cotton garments were made and stored for the blessed event. Though few everyday garments survived their

The bottom drawer is a classic place for storing precious linens. In this large chest of drawers made by my great-grandfather in 1850 for his bride, I still keep handmade linens, including crocheted coverlets, hand towels, lace-edged pillow slips, and embroidered tablecloths on acid-free tissue–covered cardboard rolls interspersed with lavender-filled sachets.

A tea tablecloth of drawn-thread work, embroidered in the 1890s by my great-aunts, hangs on the washing line.

Antique quilts displayed on a vintage wooden ladder rack.

hard use, christening robes, because they are used comparatively seldom in each generation, have endured and are much collected. In my family, we were all christened in the same robe my mother wore as an infant. My sister's sons and my daughters all wore the same robe, and I hope their children will too.

My own definition of household linens has come to include any useful fabric items needed in the general running of a house that can be folded or rolled and stored in closets or drawers. The elegant linen closet may be large or small, according to the household. Grand houses have huge cupboard-lined linen rooms where all the ironing and mending is done. A one-room apartment may have nothing more than a small drawer. Some people store guest towels on open shelves in the bathroom, stack thick terry towels in a slatted closet, and keep antique quilts hung on racks or folded in nineteenth-century quilt chests. I keep precious linens, folded around sachets of home-grown lavender or rolled in tissue paper, in a huge chest of drawers made by my great-grandfather in 1850 as a present for his bride. Blankets and down-filled coverlets may be stored in chests at the foot of a bed or packed in storage boxes under the bed. Dining-room sideboards hold damask dinner napkins, a butler's pantry holds stacks of table mats and coasters, and sometimes hatboxes full of lingerie perch on a bedroom shelf.

A beautiful, well-organized linen closet stacked with downy-soft towels, freshly laundered sheets, and lace-trimmed pillowcases is a joy to behold. The exterior of it may be a romantically shabby milk-painted country jelly cupboard or the slickest built-in, electronically opened city closet. We admire shelves of neatly piled sheets, whether immaculate

A onetime kitchen closet, made by the farming family that originally built this house, is now filled with extra bed pillows, blankets, and quilts.

white-on-white hemstitched linen, brushed flannel tartan, or cotton printed with floral bouquets. There is a skill and a method to organizing a linen closet (sometimes called a linen press) or, in grand traditional houses, the arrangement of a linen room. I hope this book will give you ideas and inspiration for both filling and organizing your linen closet, however humble.

What should the ideal linen closet contain? Here are some items I would put in my ideal closet: napkins for both casual and formal meals; place mats and tablecloths; tea towels and glass cloths for drying precious china and crystal; oven cloths and mitts; aprons; fingertip towels for guests; laundry bags and ironing board covers; flat and fitted sheets; pillowcases for standard pillows, bolsters, and European square pillows; dainty small pillowcases for decorative bed pillows and neck rolls; blanket, duvet, and mattress covers; terry towels in all sizes; bath mats; washcloths; and beach towels for the summer. Add to this list irresistible vintage embroidered linens like old-fashioned bureau scarves, mats, tray cloths, doilies, handkerchiefs, tea and egg cozies, and even hot water bottle covers. And, on the top shelf, stored in a special box that is almost never opened, a wedding dress and veil, all puffed out and cradled in tissue paper, awaiting, perhaps, the next bride in the family.

Fine old linens and laces are precious and fragile, so they are best rolled on tubes and wrapped with nonacidic tissue paper. The very house-proud German grandmother of a friend of mine died recently. She had left bottom drawers full of wonderful linens and laces, some from her 1910 trousseau from "the old country" and some more casual and colorful items from the 1940s. The napkins were all meticulously laundered and stacked in piles, tied with colored ribbons. I have known a couple so proud of their tablecloths they stored them on rollers hung from the ceiling of a linen room to ensure they were always without creases.

Few of us can keep linen rooms, closets, or drawers as tidy as that. And ultimately, unless we are collectors, it is our use of linens that is important. One way to achieve a gorgeous linen closet is to buy armloads of brand-new napkins, pristine sheets, and thick, soft towels with handsome hand-knotted fringes. But what if your budget doesn't allow for this, or none of the colors or designs available are ex-

actly what is needed for your space? What if the standard-sized tablecloth that catches your eye doesn't fit the walnut dining-room table you inherited from your great-aunt, or a store-bought mattress cover is too tight for the Edwardian brass bed you picked up at an estate sale? Or perhaps the linens you really fancy — those of the best quality found in the finest specialty stores — are far too expensive.

Luckily, many household linens can be made at home — as they always used to be in the less frenetic past. Quite easily, you can make your own bedspreads, floor-touching tablecloths, and a host of other articles, all tailored to your requirements in size, color, and style. By creating your own household linens, you can enhance your home and personalize each room in the house. You can also make wonderful, unique gifts for friends, selecting colors and fabrics to suit their needs and whims.

For those who don't have the time or inclination to make their own linens, antique linens soften and warm a room. They can save a table from dust and scratches and add a wonderful, human touch. Delectable vintage linens conjure up a time when women of the house were proud of their needle crafts. This book will discuss how to recognize quality antique linens as well as suggesting imaginative ways to use linens in your home. Perhaps that vintage bureau scarf — fifty years ago no self-respecting bedroom was without one — can embellish a bolster cover on a bed; or a precious lace panel can be hung on a simple rod across a bathroom window to filter light and give privacy; or your grandmother's hand-tatted lace doily can become the centerpiece of a boudoir pillow. There are dozens of ways to recycle the past and give rooms distinction and a welcoming atmosphere.

Guests often wonder whose portrait is cross-stitched onto this 1920s hot water bottle cover found in a thrift shop. I wish I knew.

A high kitchen cabinet in a summer cottage holds stacks of well-used drying cloths, napkins, and tablecloths, as well as candles ready for emergencies.

There is information in the source list at the back of this book about where to shop for unusual handmade linens. The source list gives specific places to find vintage linens as well as the names of fabric and findings suppliers. You will also find out how to recognize various materials and types of embroidery in vintage linens.

This book contains many ideas for designing, embellishing, sewing, finding, using, and maintaining household linens, including lots of specific instructions for projects to make. All you need is a sewing machine; simple, basic equipment; a few sewing skills; and, most of all, your imagination.

MATERIALS

*Fabrics,
Trimmings, and
Embroidery*

IN THE NINETEENTH CENTURY, beautifully starched and ironed white damask tablecloths and dinner napkins were used at every meal in the average middle- and upper-class household. Nowadays these high-maintenance linens are only used on formal occasions. Family eating habits have become casual. Heirloom table linens often remain folded in dresser drawers, while washable place mats and paper napkins have become the norm. However, many households take pride in those special times when the good linens, the best china, and well-polished silverware come out of hiding and are used with pleasure.

Today, white sales are no longer white. Since the 1920s, color has gradually crept into our table linens. At that time, small colored tablecloths with matching napkins used for luncheon, and even daintier cloths and napkins used for afternoon tea, came into general use, though earlier, special tablecloths had been embroidered in color.

Bedspreads, quilts, coverlets of all kinds, and bed hangings have long been colorful and made of a variety of fabrics. Crewel work — wool embroidery on linen or cotton, usually depicting flowers and vines — decorated bed hangings of the affluent in the late seventeenth century. Colorful (and for the first time colorfast) printed cotton *palampores* — an Indian word for a counterpane depicting a fanciful tree of life design — covered the beds of the fashionable in France in the eighteenth century. Skilled housewives in England and America sewed quilts from colored scraps in the nineteenth century that are now exhibited as works of art. Blankets, too, were frequently colorful, from distinctive American Navajo blankets to thick Hudson Bay blankets in

This English fumed oak Arts and Crafts dresser belonging to folk art collector Raymond Saroff holds a well-starched cotton damask tablecloth bordered with drawn-thread work and a hand-pulled fringed edge. In an upper drawer are printed linen napkins from the famous French company Porthault, with distinctive scalloped edges, painstakingly hand-hemmed with narrow single binding. On the floor is an American hooked rug.

PREVIOUS PAGES: A collection of traditional christening robes and children's underwear from the late nineteenth and early twentieth centuries shows some of the skills used in the making of linens.

This blue-and-white cotton damask cloth fits a small tea table. It was probably made in the late 1920s, judging from the woven design, which shows a country house and dog, and it still has appeal today, especially with classic blue-and-white china.

blue, red, or, most recognizably, multicolored stripes on cream wool. Until the twentieth century, however, intimate bed and bath linens—sheets, pillowcases, and towels—were generally white. By way of exception, it is known that as early as the sixteenth century, Francis I slept between black satin sheets.

But most sheets remained as white as possible, even when made of cotton or silk, and elaborately trimmed with lace or embroidery.

In the latter half of the twentieth century, however, a change occurred. Linens were transformed by color. In an America made prosperous by the Second World War, the house-proud wife took to color in her previously all-white kitchen, bedrooms, and bathrooms. She installed brown and avocado refrigerators, pink and blue baths, lilac and gold towels.

Embroidered, flounced, and buttoned linens are stored in an exceptionally high 1785 bow-fronted Hepplewhite-style chest of drawers designed originally for a man's use but now ideal for linens.

This awakening to color—fueled by "color psychiatrists"—included colored sheets and sheets with printed designs. I well remember the first time I saw printed sheets, in the early 1960s, when a savvy client of my husband Keith's gave him sheets scattered with a chic design of pansies.

The invention of nylon, polyester, and new fabric finishes brought the introduction of drip-dry and no-iron blends, lightening the laundry load. The sizes of sheets also changed as more and more households included queen- and king-sized beds. Bottom sheets were given shaped corners and elastic edges to fit smoothly onto mattresses. Electric blankets and heating pads took the place of hot water bottles (which in turn had long since replaced warming pans). Mattress and blanket covers, dust ruffles, and coy fluffy covers for toilet seats and tissue boxes began to appear in average homes.

Printed and colored sheets continued into the exuberant sixties, with the addition of pop, op, and Peter Max-ish designs. Black lavatories and tubs were installed in bathrooms decorated with printed silver paper. Lucite and mirrored cube tables were the rage. Instead of plain white sheets to be used inter-

Lingerie dries on the line in the middle of winter.

The nineties have brought us back to earth with leanings toward pure fibers—like Granny had in the good old days—and unbleached, undyed sheets of cotton, linen, or even hemp. The trendsetters call it "shabby chic." However, natural fibers have become somewhat of a luxury. The stylish "downsized" life requires either pure white, natural, or simple tailored shirting stripes and checks for superior quality bed linens; cashmere or cotton mesh blankets; and thick white or natural Turkish towels. But simplicity —as those two earlier arbiters of taste, Marie Antoinette and Josephine Bonaparte, discovered—is often startlingly expensive.

FABRICS

As we've seen, the term *linen* no longer refers only to real linen. Shops that specialize in "linens" sell items made of cotton, linen, silk, wool, cashmere—even rayon and ramie—and many blends of natural and man-made fibers. Discussed below are the main fiber categories for linens, their properties, and some of the fabrics made from them. Here also is a list of trimmings that are useful to know about if you are interested in making your own linens.

Though fabrics come in many different widths, depending on their place of origin, the main widths encountered in fabric stores and decorator houses are approximately 36 inches, 45 inches (both of these widths tend to be found in apparel fabrics), and 54 inches up to 60 inches (which are widths found in decorative fabric houses). There are endless exceptions, however, so adapt any of the projects in this book accordingly.

changeably on every bed, bed linens were targeted —florals for women, tough geometrics for men, and Mickey Mouse for kids—and all were coordinated to each room's decor.

In the seventies, dark purple, black, brown, and hunter green sheets were used on ubiquitous waterbeds, lit by lava lamps, and were even made of black or chocolate brown satin. In stylish bedrooms, the duvet, long a fixture in Northern Europe, made an appearance in America, as did European-sized square pillows and many varieties of bolsters and neckrolls.

In a summer cottage, casual cotton napkins are stored in a vintage leather trunk.

COTTON, grown from shrubs of the mallow family, has been cultivated in India since at least 3000 B.C. but only manufactured in Europe since the invention of mechanical processing techniques during the industrial revolution. Cotton growing in America started at the Jamestown colony in 1607 and flourished as a major commerce associated with the American South. Because the picking of cotton required intensive hand labor, it was instrumental in promoting the slave trade and its ongoing legacy.

There are many types of cotton (see the glossary for a list). Soil and climate affect the color, strength, length, and characteristics of this fiber. Cotton is the most common and versatile of all the fibers used for domestic linens, being washable, strong, and long lasting. Cotton can range in type from fine sheers to heavyweight canvas. Varieties of cotton fabric useful for making household linens include the following (for detailed definitions see the glossary): *awning stripe* (for pillows and seat pads), *batik* (great for bed-spreads), *batiste* (for sheer curtains and blanket covers), *calico* (for informal napkins and aprons), *cambric* (for table linen, handkerchiefs, church linens), *canvas* (for outdoor items), *chambray* (for aprons, shirts, curtains), *chintz* (for bedspreads, hangings, dust ruffles, and slipcovers), *crash* (for table linen and drapery), *denim* (good for making bedspreads and pillows for children's rooms or sporty, country, or ranch-style rooms), *dimity* (for slipcovers and cushions), *dotted swiss,* also known as *point d'esprit* (for vanity skirts and bed curtains), *flannel* (for interlining and sheets), *flour sacking* (reused by rural seamstresses for clothing and household linens), *gingham* (for kitchen curtains and aprons), *glass toweling* (used for drying cloths), *lawn* (for handkerchiefs and teatime aprons), *Marseilles work* (used as traditional bed covers), *muslin* (useful for making patterns when unfinished, and a multipurpose cloth when given a commercial finish), *percale* (for bed linen), *piqué* (for hand towels and blanket covers), *seersucker* (for bedspreads), *ticking* (for covers of mattresses and pillows and also, depending on the fashion, for upholstery), *terry cloth,* also known as *Turkish toweling* (for towels, facecloths, and slip-covering bathroom stools and slipper chairs), and *voile* (for blanket covers and under-curtains).

LINEN is made from a blue-flowered plant called *flax,* which is sometimes used as another name for linen. The Dutch perfected the skill of bleaching linen, done originally, according to *The Book of Fine Linen* by Françoise de Bonneville, by "soaking a piece of cloth with whey and spreading it in a meadow." Linen is produced in various countries, but the best known is from Belgium and Ireland.

When I was a child, linen was sometimes also known as *Holland cloth.* My elder sister and I wore

Holland smocks — natural linen dresses with high yokes that were hand embroidered. In retrospect, they must have been quite elegant, but at our kindergarten the other children did not understand the chic of natural-colored linen and told us they looked dirty! Holland cloth nowadays is a plain-woven linen or cotton, often heavily sized and given an oil treatment to render it opaque, and usually used for window shades.

Linen can vary in weight from lightweight *handkerchief linen* to heavy drapery weights. It is highly absorbent, soaking up water and gaining weight as it does so. Linen is guaranteed to wrinkle — though blending it with polyester lessens this property — but it looks spectacular when well ironed because of its subdued but lustrous finish. Like silk, it takes color magnificently.

Linen is often used for hand-hemstitched items

This linen dish towel, bought by my grandparents as a souvenir, was made to commemorate the 1902 coronation of Edward VII. Into the red border are woven symbols of the continents and into the cream damask are woven the names of the countries that were then part of the British Commonwealth.

because the threads pull out and can be counted readily. It is still desirable for sheets, pillowcases, tea towels (drying cloths), napery, hand-embroidered items, communion linens, and handkerchiefs, as well as articles of clothing.

Huckaback, or *huck,* is a heavy linen or cotton cloth with a honeycomb or waffle weave, used as toweling. *Hemp,* used in the past as the poor man's linen, is a coarse, tough, nonluxurious, more cotton-like fiber than linen. Now part of the back-to-the-earth movement, hemp fiber is imported because it is currently illegal to grow it in this country, as marijuana can be derived from the plant. It is used for bed linen and apparel. *Ramie* is another fiber with some of the properties of linen and hemp. It is used in decorative fabrics and apparel.

MAN-MADE FIBERS are most successful when they are blended with natural fibers. This way the pleasing look and hand of the natural fiber, be it cotton, silk, linen, or wool, is to a great extent retained, while the man-made fiber gives strength, washability, and wrinkle-free practicality to fabric. The process of blending has become sophisticated. *Rayon,* used since the 1930s, was once a cheap substitute for silk and shrank spectacularly when laundered by mistake. Now it is much in demand as a high-fashion fiber. Since World War II, when it was developed for parachutes, *nylon* has taken on many different roles. It can be used for under-curtains and as a plissé for ready-made blanket covers. The most versatile man-made fiber of all is *polyester,* introduced first in Britain, then licensed by Dupont, and now used in combination with many other fibers. *Polar fleece* is a relatively recent man-made fabric. Blankets of this can be bought ready made or the fabric purchased by the yard. *Fiberfill* is a polyester

stuffing that can be bought in various forms: in sheets to use in quilts, in small pieces to stuff into pillows, and in pillow forms. *Foam rubber* is a material that comes in many weights and thicknesses and can be used for padding and mattresses.

SILK was discovered in China as early as 2697 B.C., by the wife of Emperor Huang, according to Chinese tradition. It is a fiber formed by the silkworm—which is not a worm but a moth. *Worm* refers to the caterpillar stage of its development. Silk is made from the fine thread that forms the cocoon covering the pupa.

The extraordinary properties and beauty of silk have been apparent for centuries. It has never been inexpensive, because its production demands skilled hand labor. The Silk Route, by which the precious cargo traveled from the Far East to the West, was associated with romance and adventure. Ancient Romans were so mad for silk it became worth its weight in gold.

No other fiber takes colors quite so well. Silk can be as fine as paper-thin taffeta or as heavy as thick-piled velvet. The weight of silk is determined by the mm, pronounced "mumme," or "momme." The higher the mm, the heavier the silk. For all its beauty, silk is prone to rot and can be fragile. When we were children, a dressmaker made my sister and me nightgowns of peach-colored silk. We ruined them the first night we wore them by bouncing on the bed!

Fabrics made from silk fiber that are useful in the elegant linen closet include the following (see the glossary for detailed descriptions): *chenille* (for bed throws, coverlets, pillows, and robes) can be made of silk or a blend of silk and other fibers; *dupioni* (for coverlets and drapery), *pongee*, *tussah*, and *shantung*

FAR LEFT: *These cocktail napkins are made from Indian silk plaids. See chapter 3 for instructions on how to make them.*

LEFT: *The blanket slung over the railing of this country porch is made of a colorful wool check that reverses to plain navy melton. It is used as a lap throw and as an extra bed blanket.*

RIGHT: *A selection of white and natural-colored trimmings include block, tassel, and fan-edged fringe, rope, cord, lace, and crochet.*

(see the glossary) are now fairly interchangeable terms for lightweight, natural-colored silk (used for robes); *organza* (for sheer curtains and dainty aprons); *ottoman* (for pillows and welting) can be of silk or of a silk and cotton blend; *rep* and *tie silks* (for robes); *satin* (for glamorous sheets and pillowcases, padded coverlets, robes, and lingerie); crepe de chine (for nightgowns and lingerie); and *taffeta* (for curtains, bed drapery, and petticoats).

Now polyester, which does not require the upkeep of silk, is used to duplicate many of these fabrics. But real silk, like handmade lace, has a precious, unique quality.

WOOL, made from sheep shearings, has always been used for warmth, especially for blankets. Wool almost never survives long enough to become heirloom because it is so prone to the ravages of moths. Each culture and maker or manufacturer has its own distinctive type of blanket. Often robes are also made by blanket makers. Some classic edgings to finish blankets include blanket stitching and satin or grosgrain ribbon edging.

Various types of wool include the following (see the glossary for detailed descriptions): *cashmere* (ideal for luxurious throws and blankets), *felt* (for handicraft projects, pads for tables or rugs, and as trimming), *melton* (used for blankets as well as garments), *wool flannel* (for blankets), and *mohair* (for blankets and throws).

TRIMMINGS

Trimmings can be applied to fabrics to personalize, embellish, and coordinate household linens to a room. The main categories of trimmings are braids, cording, fringes, gimps, ribbons, and welting. *Braids* can be one-eighth of an inch up to four inches wide and come in many weaves and colors. Braids are generally flat in shape, though they are often textured. *Cording* is twisted or plaited and comes in a number of sizes and variations. Cord can be either applied to or, if sewn to a tape, inserted into upholstery and cushion edges to add color and definition. When cording is over an inch in diameter, it is often called *rope. Fringes* can be found in many variations (see glossary for more detail), such as *ball* or *bobble* fringe, *beaded* fringe, *block* fringe, *bullion* fringe, *fan-edge* fringe, also called *giselle, knotted* fringe (found on good Turkish bath towels), *moss* fringe, sometimes called *brush* fringe, *self* fringe, and *tassel* fringe. *Gimp,* a flat, narrow woven trimming, comes in a variety of raised designs and is used on wood-frame furniture and in decorative ways on shelves, the edges of lamp shades, and pillows. *Ribbon* is woven on a loom and can vary from one-eighth of an inch to five or more inches wide. The most useful type is grosgrain, which is both a ribbed fabric and a ribbon that comes in many sizes and colors.

Welting, also called piping, can be bought ready made in a limited number of colors or can be made at home (see chapter 3) by trapping filler cord in a bias strip of fabric. Welting cord and fillers are needed for making welting (piping) to give a professional finish to many household items, such as place mats and pillows. Filler cord of various widths ranging from an eighth of an inch to an inch in diameter can be found in craft shops and upholstery supply shops. For very thin piping, use one strand or several strands of cotton household string. Prefabricated welting can be bought from upholstery supply stores, but it is usually sold in packages on cards rather than by the yard.

EMBROIDERY

The term *embroidery* refers to ornamental needlework worked with thread on fabric. Many queens, princesses, and well-born ladies, such as Elizabeth I, Mary, Queen of Scots, Catherine de Medici, and Marguerite de Valois, were skilled embroiderers.

There are many ways of embellishing fabric with applied white or colored thread. Originally always done by hand, much embroidery now is duplicated on a schiffli or other type of machine. However, nothing can beat the look — whether sophisticated or charmingly artless — of hand embroidery.

There are many types of embroidery. *Appliqué* is embroidery done when one fabric is cut into a shape and applied — often with fancy stitches — to another fabric to form a design. Some commercial appliqués with adhesive backing can be set in place with a hot iron. *Beadwork* is worked by sewing tiny

This circular linen tablecloth was embroidered by my great-aunts to their own design around 1870. The technique is cutwork, with some surface embroidery and a tatted fringe.

This fingertip towel with cherubs features a type of colbert embroidery worked by my great-aunts in the 1880s.

glass beads onto a grid of canvas like needlepoint and can be used on pillows, footstools, pincushions, and bell pulls. *Colbert* embroidery is worked with thread on a net or mesh ground.

Crewel is wool embroidery, usually on linen, often depicting flowers, vines, and animals. It is used extensively on bed hangings and pillows. *Cutwork* is usually worked white on white on cotton or linen. Shapes are cut out, then finished around the raw edges with a closely packed buttonhole stitch. The effect is lacelike but in fact is embroidery (see the photograph on page 20). *Drawnwork,* also called *hemstitching* or *fagoting,* is made by pulling threads out of fine linen, then reassembling the threads in groups to form a ladderlike design, or twisting them into more elaborate designs that can be horizontal and vertical, with various knottings of threads in between (as seen on the breakfast tray and bedside

This well-preserved nineteenth-century quilt uses appliqués and motifs padded with cotton stuffing to achieve its effect. (Collection of Raymond Saroff.)

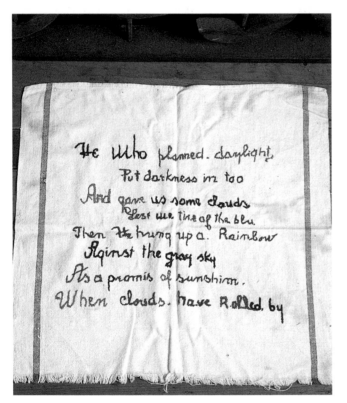

This poem, with all its imperfections, was touchingly embroidered in a crude form of satin stitch on a worn-out drying cloth in the 1940s by Ella Kruger, a German woman who lived in the Catskills. (Collection of Raymond Saroff.)

table on page 132). *Eyelet* embroidery (called *broderie Anglaise* in England and France) was originally made by punching holes in fine white cotton with a stiletto and oversewing with packed stitches around the holes to form repeating designs. Now eyelet is made by machine. Its main characteristic is the little round or oval holes, though surface embellishments often connect the holes. Eyelet is most typically white on white. It is useful for small café curtains, boudoir pillows, dust ruffles, and bed hangings. *Needlepoint* is worked with yarn—usually wool—on a mesh canvas using a blunted needle. Stitches include *bargello* and *cross-stitch*—called *gros point* or *petit point,* according to size. *Patchwork* is made by joining several different fabrics, usually to form a larger pattern. There are hundreds of variations with colorful, folksy names, and many different techniques, including appliqué, surface embroidery, and *trapunto.*

Quilting is closely allied to patchwork; it is the process that joins a plain or patchwork fabric to a lining fabric with a padded interfacing between. To make large quilts in the past, women often gathered around a quilting frame and held a quilting bee, all stitching on the same quilt. Now quilting can be produced by special machines. *Smocking* is done on lightweight fabric that is gathered in even rows, then embroidered with decorative surface stitches that hold and stabilize the gathers. Though most popular on little girls' dresses, it is also used as headings on curtains and bed draperies, and on lamp shades and nightgowns. *Trapunto* is a type of linear quilting formed by trapping soft cord between parallel lines of stitching. Quilts with three-dimensional puffed and padded work are often called "trapunto," but generally this term refers to corded, filled designs rather than puffs, which is more related to the Elizabethan term *stump work* or the nineteenth-century term *Berlin work.*

Surface stitches used in embroidery include: *backstitch, chain stitch, cross-stitch, featherstitch, French knots* and *bullion knots, herringbone stitch, lazy daisy stitch, running stitch, satin stitch,* and many more. For some descriptions of sewing techniques for embroidery, see chapter 8.

Lace encompasses a large variety of techniques, most of them nowadays being done by machines. A handy definition of lace is that it is openwork fabric or edging formed from thread, cut and embroidered, or made of woven tape or ribbon to give an open effect. Laces were originally handmade and acquired their names from the areas where they were first made. The minute variations and imperfections make handmade lace interesting and much collected. In the listing below, I include crochet and tatting because they too are formed from a single thread, though the effect is different from most lace.

The varieties of lace include *point lace,* made from thread by needle, such as *Alençon* lace, *guipure,* and *venise* lace; *pillow lace,* made on a pillow using bobbins, such as *Chantilly, Cluny, Nottingham,* and *Valenciennes* (Val); *crocheted lace,* such as *Irish* lace; lace made with woven ribbons, such as *Renaissance* lace; lace appliquéd to net, such as *Brussels* and *Normandy* lace; *schiffli* embroidery, which originated in Switzerland (*schiffli* means "boat" and refers to the shape of the shuttle on a schiffli machine); lace darned in squares onto a mesh ground, such as *filet* lace; and *tatting,* fine, spider's-web effects made from thread worked by hand using a special double-pointed bobbin.

A selection of white lace trimmings gathered in a basket.

A tablecloth of thick, encrusted lace looks somewhat bridal on this eighteenth-century Italian statue depicting Spring.

SEWING EQUIPMENT AND TECHNIQUES

T HE HOUSEHOLD that takes pride in its linens usually has the basic equipment needed to make and maintain them. The essentials include needles, thread, scissors, sewing machine, and an iron and ironing board. These and other tools needed to create linens are described below.

SCISSORS AND OTHER CUTTING TOOLS

A pair of sharp scissors is the first requirement. You can get by with one medium-sized pair of scissors. For cutting fabric, shears, which have longer and stronger blades than regular scissors, are used by professionals because they are more efficient. For cutting straight lines, many home sewers like to use a rotary cutter with a mat. Always keep a pair of fairly small scissors next to the sewing machine when sewing, to clip threads and make tiny notches. Make sure all scissors are sharpened periodically. There are few things more frustrating than trying to cut fabric with dull scissors.

Optional cutting equipment includes a pair of pinking shears for finishing the inside of certain seams or for decorative edging. A leather punch is

Fabric remnants are stored in stacks by color in a cupboard. The small vintage sewing machine is French, made around 1870; it makes a chain stitch. The larger machine is contemporary.

PREVIOUS PAGES: *Simple flat, self-covered buttons with two or four holes were a classic type of button used on domestic linens in the nineteenth and first half of the twentieth centuries.*

In my workroom, which is used for writing, painting, and drawing as well as sewing, I have a vinyl-topped cutting table. I had it made on a hinge so it can be folded up against the wall with the legs tucked into it when it is not in use. The polished wood sewing box in the background was my grandmother's. I still use it.

Up until the 1950s, pillowcases and other household linens were often fastened with washable buttons covered in criss-crossed threads like those shown here.

useful for making small round holes, as is a stiletto, which is used for making the holes in eyelet embroidery. Cutting knives with replaceable blades, such as Exacto knives, are useful in many craft projects.

Foldaway aluminum tables are useful as cutting tables, especially when cutting large pieces of cloth; two placed together give reasonable cutting space.

FASTENERS

Ties, lacings, and buttons were some of the earliest types of fastenings, and all are still in use today. Always save the buttons and buckles when you throw out a garment and keep them in a button bag.

On fancy linens, mother-of-pearl buttons look wonderful but may break if professionally laundered. Their plastic equivalents are less breakable,

though they do not have quite the same luxurious effect. Self-covered buttons can be useful, and button molds to make these are found in most fabric and craft stores. Recently there has been a trend toward wooden buttons on casual linens.

It is useful to have several sizes of snap fasteners and hooks and eyes always on hand, but zippers can be bought as needed for upholstery projects or pillows.

One of the most useful fasteners is Velcro. It can be used on slipcovers, bathroom sink skirts, inside picnic baskets (such as the one on page 113), and on many other items. If you are making outdoor pillows, for instance the mitered striped ones on page 105, use Velcro, as it will not deteriorate, rust, or jam as a zipper would and is totally washable.

IRON AND IRONING BOARD

Most households have an electric iron and ironing board. It takes skill to iron properly. When I went to school, the boys learned woodworking and the girls domestic science. The whole of the first lesson was spent learning to iron a handkerchief correctly, using a flatiron heated on a stove. Handkerchiefs and flatirons are both considered quaint now, but I have never forgotten the lesson and apply it frequently, dampening cotton and linen, testing the heat of the iron with a wet finger, and ironing the tiny hems on the wrong side first.

It is important to use an iron continually as you sew. Every seam should be pressed as it is stitched to keep the work smooth. Pressing and pinning hems before they are stitched saves time. Small ironing boards and sleeve boards are useful for tiny projects, and they take up little space. If you are using velvet or any fabric with a plushy pile, it is best to use a needle board when you iron, as it prevents the pile from being crushed.

MARKING TOOLS

Fabric must be cut accurately in order to save a lot of time sewing. This means the shapes must be marked clearly on the fabric. Professional cutters use tailor's chalk or tailor's wax, which comes in slender white, red, black, or yellow oblongs that can be sharpened with the blade of a pair of scissors to keep the line fine. A well-sharpened pencil or contrasting colored pencil may be used instead of tailor's chalk or wax. When marking batting, a ballpoint pen is efficient, as it runs smoothly along the surface.

Mark the fabric on the wrong side whenever possible in case of mistakes that cannot be erased. If you are using a printed fabric that has to be carefully placed and the pattern cannot be discerned from the wrong side, mark on the right side, but very lightly. Tailor's wax can be melted and removed with a hot iron and a paper towel. There is a continually changing variety of erasable marking pencils to be found in craft stores.

MEASURING EQUIPMENT

A crisp new tape measure is an essential for all domestic linen projects. Old ones wear out and cannot be relied on for accuracy. Be sure to get a tape measure with inches on one side and centimeters on the other, as more and more of the world is turning to the decimal system.

A wooden yardstick is good for large amounts of fabric and for cutting bias piping if needed. Make sure the yardstick is perfectly straight — with age, wooden rulers tend to warp. A twelve-inch ruler, a set square, and a protractor are useful but not essential. A metal right-angled ruler is useful for cutting accurately. In a pinch, a right angle can be established by setting anything rectangular, such as a book or magazine, against the selvage of the fabric and drawing a horizontal line against it.

PINS AND ODD BUT USEFUL ITEMS

Always have on hand a box or pincushion full of clean, sharp pins. To keep pins and needles for hand sewing nearby while you are machining, wrap thick fabric such as felt around the "waist" of your sewing machine as an improvised pincushion. A bracelet pincushion keeps pins and needles handy when you are cutting or hand sewing. If you cannot find one at your local craft store, sew a wide elastic band cut to fit around your wrist and sew onto it a regular pincushion.

Flat Pincushion

When we were children, we made simple pincushions from cardboard, covered first in flannel, then in fabric. The flannel makes them soft enough to hold needles and safety pins. I still have one in use that I made as a child. Try to pick fabric that is precious or interesting, or that relates to the shape of the pincushion. As it does not have to be washable, silk or brocaded fabric is fine. It can be attractive to make several pincushions that relate in color but are different shapes, such as those shown on page 30.

Materials (for one pincushion)
- 2 small remnants of fabric about 6 in. (15.2 cm) square
- 2 6-in. (15.2 cm) pieces of paper card, such as firm cereal-box or shirt cardboard
- 2 6-in. (15.2 cm) scraps of brushed cotton flannel or other padding
- Straight pins, plain and with colored knobs (if desired)

You Will Also Need
Marking pencil, ruler, scissors, sewing needle, matching thread

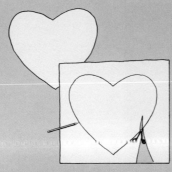

1. Cut cardboard.
From cardboard, cut two pieces from 3 to 5 in. (7.6 to 12.7 cm) across in such simple shapes as square, circle, oval, heart, or octagon.

2. Cover with flannel.
Lay single card on flannel and cut two pieces about ¾ in. (19.1 mm) larger than card shape. If sewing heart shape, cut deep notch at top.

Thread needle with double thread and large knot. Attach flannel pieces tightly onto each card, taking stitches from opposite sides of shape and pulling tightly.

WRONG SIDE OF FABRIC

3. Sew fabric to cards.
Lay flannel-covered shapes on wrong side of fabric, smooth flannel sides down. Select best places for design; see, for instance, heart-shaped pincushion in photograph below, with cherubs placed in design. Cut roughly ¾ in. (19.1 mm) larger than shapes. As with flannel, cover shapes so right sides are smooth.

4. Sew both cards together.
Taking tiny overcast stitches, sew both padded, fabric-covered pieces together.

5. Place pins.
Place pins—regular dressmaker pins and colored-head pins if desired—all around edge of pincushion so they slot between the two pieces of card. On front of pincushion, place various sizes of needles and safety pins.

Pins can be kept in pretty and decorative pin holders such as these three, handmade from printed linen, a red-on-white toile, and an allover printed cotton.

Millinery and upholstery pins are longer, stronger, and have bent T-shaped ends. They are useful for projects in which length or strength is needed, such as padded items.

For turning tabs or fine piping right side out, use a knitting needle or chopstick, or get a long, fine professional turner with a hook at the end. To keep needles from rusting, use emery in a bag or an emery board.

SEWING MACHINE

To make any of the following projects, you will need a sewing machine and some practice at using it. There are many varieties available, but the one you use does not have to be the latest model: I use a heavy, steel-based machine that is forty years old, and my sister uses one that belonged to our grand-mother — so old it has cylindrical bobbins and a handle that is turned by hand! But both machines are perfectly adequate for all the following projects. There are now available computerized machines that can work wonders, including embroidery and even monograms. However, most people who sew have simpler lightweight sewing machines with a zigzag stitch capability that is useful for finishing seams, doing appliqué work, and making button-holes. Special feet can be attached for gathering, hemming, and other operations. A zipper foot is an *absolute* essential, necessary for making welting as well as setting zippers, because it enables the ma-chine needle to stitch right up close to the welting cord. Some zipper feet are adjustable and can be used on the right or left side of the zipper or welting. Others can be purchased either left or right ori-ented. Some fabrics, such as leather or fabrics with a thick pile, are easier to sew on a machine using a Teflon-coated foot or a rolling foot. Most of the work described in this book is done by machine, but some hand stitching is recommended when certain household linens are embroidered or need repair.

SEWING NEEDLES

Always have on hand various weights of sewing machine needles. You will probably use a size 14 needle — the average size — most of the time, but sometimes you will be using layers of heavy fabric, perhaps together with bulky cording, and your sewing machine may balk at the thickness, especially where heavy cording overlaps. For heavyweight fabric, always use a heavyweight size 16 or even an 18 needle. If that needle breaks, consider hand stitching the thickest parts as an alternative to machine stitching. A size 11, a fine needle, is best for sheer fabrics.

Also have on hand several sizes and weights of hand sewing needles. When making anything of fur or leather, use leather needles, which are specially sharpened to cut through the skin while stitching. Sometimes curved upholstery needles are necessary for certain household projects. Heavy straight upholstery needles are needed for tufted upholstery — fabric held by buttons, bows, or rosettes.

To repair needlepoint, use the appropriately sized needlepoint needle. These have blunted points so as to pass through needlepoint canvas without splitting the fibers. To repair beadwork on antique embroidery, use a very fine beading needle.

THIMBLE

Professional stitchers *always* wear thimbles for hand sewing. Find one that fits and get used to wearing it, or you will wear out the end of your middle finger.

THREAD

Keep a collection of as many shades of thread as you can so you have plenty to choose from. It pays to match your threads accurately, because you will often have to topstitch or sink a stitch close to welting on certain items. The glamour of your project will be lost if the thread is mismatched. Upholsterers usually use heavier thread than those used in

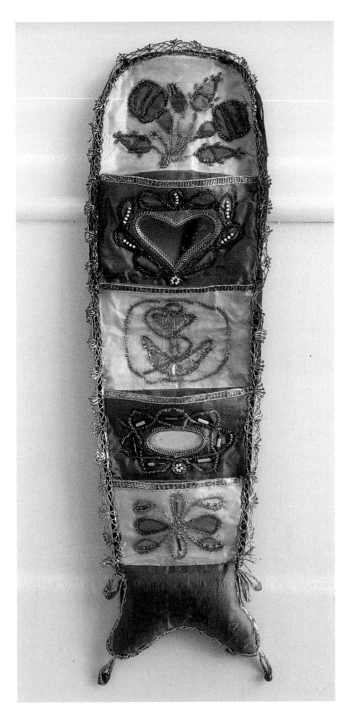

This fish-shaped object is a sewing kit made by a sailor in the nineteenth century. It can be rolled up or hung on the wall. There is a stuffed pad for pins and needles, pockets, and a mirror.

making clothing, but it is not essential. If you need to use thicker thread for strength or for an effect, use double thread. Buy an extra spool and run one spool from the top of the machine and another from the spindle used to hold the spool when winding thread onto the bobbin. Thread the machine using both strands as if one, threading the needle with both. The bobbin underneath will be a single thread.

For certain projects, a monofilament thread is best. It is almost invisible, but it does spring about a bit, making it slightly less manageable than regular cotton thread.

WEIGHTS

These are needed to hold cloth in place when cutting, especially when working with large amounts or several layers of cloth. Though professional workrooms use metal weights, many other objects will do, such as large smooth stones, books, or heavy paperweights.

Sewing Techniques and Definitions

GRAIN is important when cutting fabric. If the grain is not cut accurately projects will always look slightly tilted. "Down the grain" refers to the true direction of the vertical threads that make up cloth. A quick way to establish a true vertical grain is to run the point of a pin down the grain between two threads, forming a slight groove. Or measure in from the edge of the fabric in two separate places to establish a vertical grain line. To establish the true horizontal grain—also known as the cross grain— pull a thread from selvage to selvage, then cut along the line where the thread has been pulled. Beware

of printed designs—checks in particular—because they may not be printed on the exact cross grain.

The bias of a fabric is at a forty-five-degree angle to the selvage. It may also be referred to as "on the cross." True bias is required for making welting, and for binding that will be used on curves, such as scallops.

PILE refers to the fuzzy surface of velvet and similar fabrics. It is important to establish the direction of the pile when using velvet or velveteen. There is a big difference between the look of a pile brushed up and brushed down. Generally speaking, with the pile brushed up, the effect is richer; brushed down, the effect is lighter and dustier. Choose the direction of the pile depending on the effect you are after. Make sure the pile matches at all seams.

When machine sewing seams in velvet, pin first, placing the pins across the seam so the foot can pass over them. Pull the bottom fabric more firmly than the top fabric, as the pile of velvet tends to make the upper fabric "grow." The higher the pile, the more the velvet moves.

MATCHING is exceedingly important when using expensive patterned fabric. Matching the design at seams is one of the biggest hurdles for amateur stitchers. Always spend time deciding where to center the design. If it looks off center, the effect will be amateurish.

SEAMS

There are several methods of finishing seams in household linens, all of which are meant to enable seams to stand up to frequent laundering without raveling.

Bound seams are pressed open and each edge bound using single binding, such as commercial ready-pressed bias binding, or by using doubled-

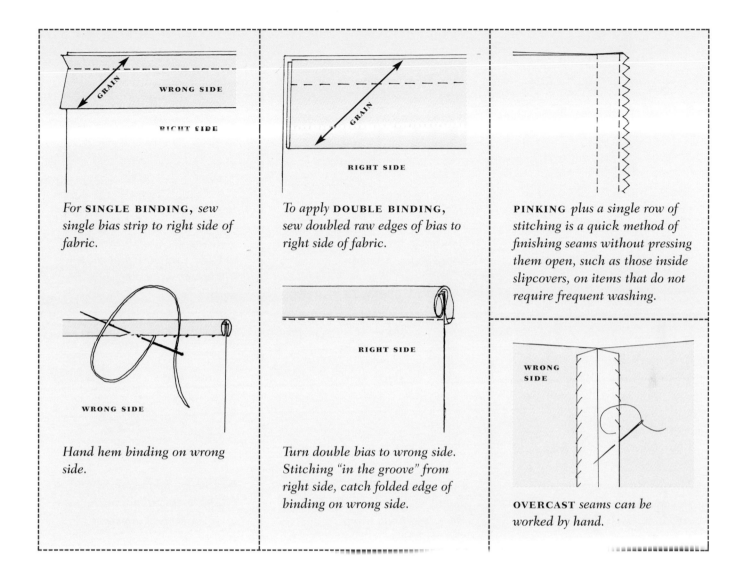

For **SINGLE BINDING,** *sew single bias strip to right side of fabric.*

Hand hem binding on wrong side.

To apply **DOUBLE BINDING,** *sew doubled raw edges of bias to right side of fabric.*

Turn double bias to wrong side. Stitching "in the groove" from right side, catch folded edge of binding on wrong side.

PINKING *plus a single row of stitching is a quick method of finishing seams without pressing them open, such as those inside slipcovers, on items that do not require frequent washing.*

OVERCAST *seams can be worked by hand.*

over bias binding, which requires no hand hemming but is heavier.

Pinking is a quick way to finish off seams but eventually will ravel. Simply stitching the seam edges, singly when pressed open or sewing the seams together, then pinking will make the seams last somewhat longer.

Overcast seams are usually pressed open and each raw edge over-stitched. They can be worked by hand or by using a zigzag attachment on a sewing ma-

chine. Professionals use a special overcasting machine called a Merrow machine.

Shirt seams are also called flat fell or run-and-fell seams. Sometimes they are called double-needle seams because when they are sewn commercially, the machine makes the seams in one operation using two needles. The home sewer usually makes this type of seam in two stitched operations.

Open turned and topstitched seams are made by pressing open seams, turning each seam allowance

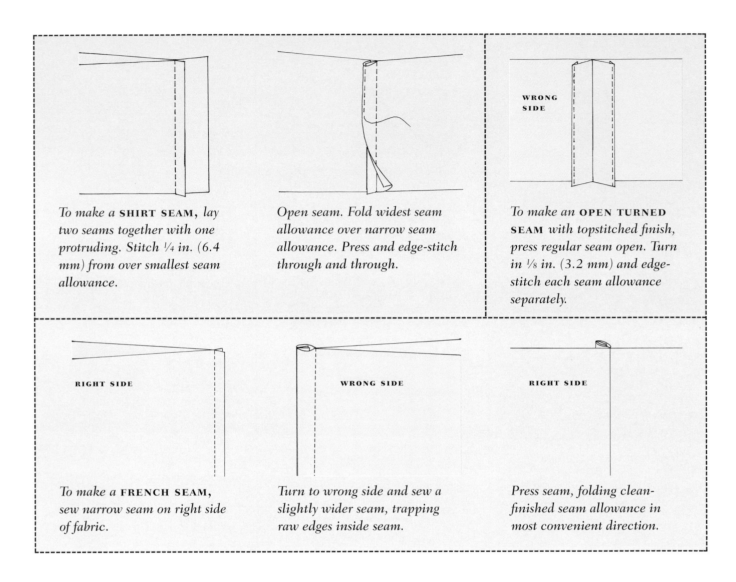

To make a **SHIRT SEAM**, lay two seams together with one protruding. Stitch ¼ in. (6.4 mm) from over smallest seam allowance.

Open seam. Fold widest seam allowance over narrow seam allowance. Press and edge-stitch through and through.

To make an **OPEN TURNED SEAM** with topstitched finish, press regular seam open. Turn in ⅛ in. (3.2 mm) and edge-stitch each seam allowance separately.

To make a **FRENCH SEAM**, sew narrow seam on right side of fabric.

Turn to wrong side and sew a slightly wider seam, trapping raw edges inside seam.

Press seam, folding clean-finished seam allowance in most convenient direction.

toward the wrong side, and topstitching.

French seams are made by first sewing a narrow seam on the right side of the fabric, then turning to the wrong side and sewing a slightly wider seam, thus trapping the raw edges inside the second seam.

WELTING

Many household linen projects require the addition of a welt, which is sometimes referred to as piping. To make welting, cut strips of fabric on the bias, join them into one continual strip, then trap filler cord in the bias strip using a zipper foot (see illustrations next page). To establish the width of the bias strips, measure around the welting filler cord and add one inch for seam allowances.

As a resource for less experienced sewers, I've included in chapter 8 instructions for all of the basic and some of the decorative stitches needed for the projects in this book. A step-by-step guide to making buttonholes will also be found there.

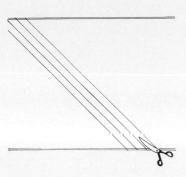

1. To make **WELTING**, first cut bias strips.

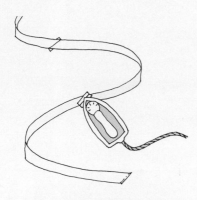

2. Join bias strips into one continual strip. The seams will be on the straight grain but will appear on the diagonal. Press seams open.

3. Lay cord in center of bias strip and, using zipper foot, stitch as closely to entrapped cord as possible.

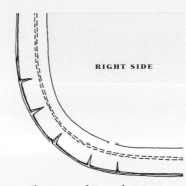

RIGHT SIDE

4. Sew welting in place, clipping seams at corners or curves.

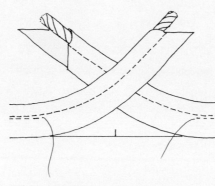

5. Though welt ends can be overlapped to finish, a better finish is to join welt ends into a continuous tube. Overlap welts 2 in. (5.1 cm) before cutting ends.

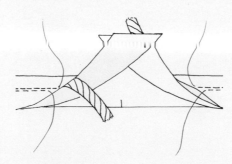

6. Open stitching on each welt end, exposing filler. Separate bias strips from filler. Pin seam joining welt fabric on straight grain (seam will appear on slant). Cut away excess turnings.

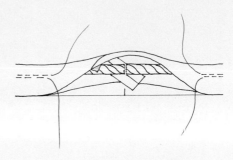

7. Sew ¼ in. (6.4 mm) seam. Press seam open. Cut filler so ends butt.

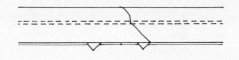

8. Reenclose filler in bias welt fabric and stitch final stretch of completed welt in place using zipper foot. If applying welting cord into a surface seam rather than at an edge seam— such as onto the front of a pillow— stitch "in the groove" between welt and fabric to keep stitches as invisible as possible.

FRONT ROOMS

Dining Rooms, Living Rooms, and Studies

ROOMS AT THE FRONT OF THE house, the front hall, living room, and dining room, are usually the rooms first seen by visitors. These rooms tend to be formal—rooms on their best behavior.

Living rooms were called parlors in Victorian times and were very proper indeed. Some were double parlors; at times one would be used by the women and one by the men. They were also known as drawing rooms—from the term "withdrawing room"—or as sitting rooms. Young girls and women showed off their needle skills in any number of ways in these front rooms, from samplers that were hung on walls to embroidered mats that protected the surfaces of small tables. When upholstered furniture became more available in the mid- to late nineteenth century, pretty lace-edged antimacassars covered the high backs of arm chairs. Lace curtains were hung at the windows. Nowadays in a well-dressed entrance hall or living room, you might find circular table skirts, cloths for a drink tray, or a table runner and cocktail napkins.

The dining room, however, is the front room in which we use the most linens today. Linens were used at feast and banquet tables long before dining tables became permanent fixtures in a household.

OPPOSITE: *Included in elegant linen closets of the past would be summer curtains, such as these lace ones by Mimi Findlay Antiques, shown at the Edith Wharton show-house in 1992. (Photo by Dennis Krukowski.)*

PREVIOUS PAGES: *This table is set for an intimate dinner in a country house. A variety of cotton tartan napkins are rolled into silver rings. Eighteenth-century Wedgwood plates sit on place mats from Madeira. (Photo by Alex McLean for* Design Times.*)*

Small linen napkins embroidered with drawnwork and satin stitch are ready for cocktails in this New York entrance hall.

In the Middle Ages, tablecloths reached all the way to the floor in order to disguise the crude trestle tables that were set up for special occasions and dismantled to clear the great hall later. Tablecloths were essential to create the most impressive, sumptuous effect.

Sometimes tablecloths were ironed into decorative creases, vertically, horizontally, or in both directions, giving a textural effect of squares. The corners of tablecloths were occasionally tied in knots, both to hold them in place and for a decorative effect. Some tablecloths were elaborate, made of silk with gold thread embroidery. Others were edged with wide bands of elaborate hand-worked lace or long knotted fringes.

In the Middle Ages guests used the tablecloth to wipe their lips. Napkins did not make an appearance until later and were originally large enough to tie around the eater's neck. Later they were hung from a buttonhole. I remember my father tucking a napkin into his clerical collar. Now napkins sit demurely on the lap.

A hand-embroidered tray cloth, worked in cross-stitch, protects a high table topped with a tray that holds drinks.

The wooden surface of a butler's tray holding silver mugs is protected by a simple linen drawn-thread tray cloth.

In this vintage copy of Mrs. Beeton's Book of Household Management *illustrations show how to set tables properly. The damask tablecloth in front shows color — still cautiously pale — creeping into linens. Individual silver rings are used to identify napkins.*

OPPOSITE: *Afternoon tea is set on a tablecloth embroidered in cross-stitch. The sampler with a sentimental quotation, also in cross-stitch, was embroidered in the 1920s by my aunt Louie.*

The embellishment of napery, as table linens were called, gave rise to the development of the lace-making and hand embroidery trades. As the middle class grew in the nineteenth century, a room set aside just for dining increasingly became a permanent feature in the family dwelling. Sideboards or dressers took the place of large buffets. China was often displayed in glass-fronted cupboards. Chairs were positioned around a central table — rather than set back against the wall — with armchairs at either end as an extra fillip of honor.

Dinner tablecloths in my mother's day were usually white damask, and there were plenty of skilled launderers to keep them starched and ironed! Gradually as the twentieth century progressed, colors crept in to all forms of napery, starting with red or blue cross-stitch embroidery for less formal luncheons or afternoon tea.

In a more relaxed time, afternoon tea was a welcome respite — in England, everything stopped for tea. Afternoon tea tablecloths tend to be dainty, with small napkins. High tea, or supper, tablecloths might be more rugged — checked, or striped seersucker, or printed cotton — and never grand at all. (Incidentally, high tea, a term often misused by Americans, does not mean a grand tea; it is the British working family's supper and consists of a savory course swilled down with pots of tea!)

In a 1909 copy of that fount of domestic information, *Mrs. Beeton's Book of Household Management* — versions of which are still in print — can be found color illustrations of tables correctly dressed for breakfast, luncheon, tea, supper, a buffet for a ball, and a dinner *à la Russe,* plus four variations of invalid trays. In the gala settings, garlands of flowers drape the corners or hang down the sides of the

Improvise napkin rings in a casual setting by writing names on wooden clothespins.

tablecloths, and little pink silk shades hide the tops of the candles. Each arrangement, however, is always based on a well-starched and ironed damask tablecloth or an embroidered white tray cloth. Mrs. Beeton also instructs us in seventeen ways to fold "serviettes," though even she admits these elaborate and fanciful foldings were slightly out of style. Instead, to quote Mrs. Beeton, napkins "in ordinary family use...are folded smoothly and slipped through napkin rings made of silver, ivory or bone." Always buy good white vintage napkins when you see them in antique shops. They will eventually wear out, but they are still the most satisfactory napkins to use.

The formality of the past has been superseded today by far more casual meals for all but the most official dinner parties. Recently there has been a fashion at dinner parties for several smaller tables — seating six or eight each — in a large dining room rather than one large table to which extra leaves are added. Tablecloths may be colorful. Napkins and

rings may be coordinated, not for identification as in the past, but to enhance the color scheme. My husband and I were once given as gifts napkin rings worked in tartan needlepoint with each individually designed ring spelling out a letter from our surname. I've seen designers in show-house dining rooms invent unusual napkin rings from silk flowers, shells, or pearls to use with ephemeral napkins made of gossamer-like cloth of gold.

There is no reason that anyone with average skill with a sewing machine cannot make pretty napkins. You do not need silver napkin rings — or the bother of polishing them — because you can make your own.

The napkin shown on page 44 is a cotton printed with a small provincial paisley motif. The ring is made from ottoman, a silky fabric with a pronounced rib. To make it more luxuriously three dimensional, a piece of batting was placed inside, but this touch is optional. An applied ribbon braid picks up the colors in the napkin.

Winter Napkins and Napkin Rings

A general rule when cutting dinner napkins is that they should be no smaller than 16 inches square. You can get three decently sized napkins across 54- to 60-inch (1.37 to 1.53 m) wide fabric, two from 36-inch (91.5 cm) fabric, and two generously sized napkins across 45-inch (1.14 m) fabric. Breakfast and tea napkins can be smaller, and cocktail napkins can be only 6 inches square —or oblong. Measurements given here are for six napkins.

Materials
- 2 yd. (1.83 m) of 50-in. (1.27 m) printed cotton
- ⅛ yd. (11.5 cm) ottoman for napkin rings
- 1½ yd. (1.37 m) of ⅞ in. (2.3 cm) ribbon or braid
- ⅛ yd. thin batting (if desired)

You Will Also Need
Ruler, marking pencil, tape measure, scissors, sewing machine, matching thread, sewing needle, iron and ironing board

1. Cut and sew napkins.
Cut six 25-in. (63.6 cm) squares. Press in tiny hems and sew by machine. If preferred, use a hem-making attachment.

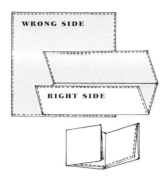

Triple-fold a napkin in both directions, then roll.

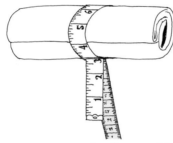

Measure around roll to establish napkin ring size. Napkin shown measures 7 in. (17.9 cm) around.

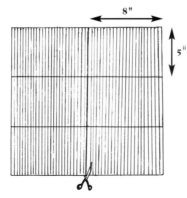

2. Cut and sew napkin rings.
Cut six rectangles 5 in. (14 cm) by

8 in. (20.4 cm) (or the measurement around your napkin roll plus 1 in. for turning) from ottoman, with ridges running vertically.

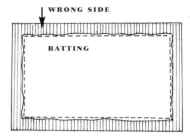

If desired, cut batting at 4 in. (10.3 cm) by 7 in. (17.8 cm) (or the measurement around your roll). Lay batting in center of wrong side of ottoman and edge-stitch both together in place. Stitching will be hidden inside ring.

Fold ottoman in half lengthwise, right sides facing. Stitch along raw edges, taking ¼ in. (6.4 mm) seams. Do not stitch ends.

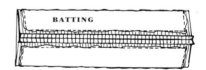

Open and center seam, then press seam open. Turn ring right side out.

(continued on following page)

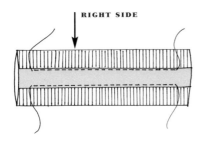

RIGHT SIDE

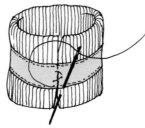

3. Add ribbon trimming.

Cut ribbon or braid same length as napkin ring (8 in.). Lay ottoman ring on flat space, seam centered and facing down. Lay ribbon through middle of ottoman. Topstitch in place with matching thread. Stop ¾ in. (19.1 mm) from either end so that seams can be turned in to finish.

4. Finishing.

Thread needle with matching thread. Carefully slip-stitch edges together, starting with crucial part, which is where ribbon ends butt. Work slip-stitches all around, even though slightly awkward, outside and inside. Repeat with other five rings.

These napkins, made of a warm red-and-green Provençal print, are given a more formal look with napkin rings made of red ottoman trimmed in ribbon braid.

Summer Napkins and Napkin Rings

If you are nervous about making the covered buttonholes for these napkin rings—which is not difficult to do—simply sew the buttons permanently in place.

Measurements given are for six generously sized dinner napkins—23 inches (58.5 cm) square—and rings. If you prefer smaller napkins, divide the width of the fabric into thirds instead of in half. (For instructions on how to make a matching bib, see chapter 5.)

Materials

- 2¼ yd. (2.57 m) of 45 in. (1.14 m) wide printed cotton for napkins
- ¼ yd. (22.9 cm) solid fabric for rings
- 3 yd. (2.74 m) welting *or* ¼ yd. (22.9 cm) solid fabric and 3 yd. (2.74 m) welting filler cord
- 6 large buttons

You Will Also Need

Ruler, marking pencil, tape measure, sewing machine with zipper foot, matching thread, sewing needle, iron and ironing board

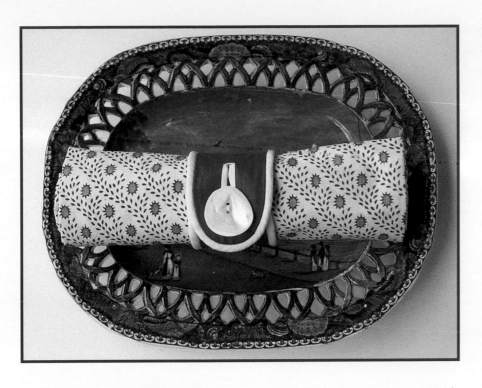

For summer, a French blue-and-white Provençal print napkin was teamed with a ring of blue polished cotton trimmed in white. A natural shell button completes the effect.

1. Cut and sew napkins.

Cut six 25-in. (63.5 cm) squares. Press narrow hems all around. Sew hems. (If preferred, use hem attachment.) Triple-fold napkins in both directions, as in instructions for Winter Napkins (page 43), then roll. Measure around roll to establish length of napkin ring (will be approximately 5½ in. [14 cm]).

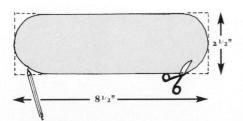

2. Cut napkin ring.

On wrong side of napkin ring fabric, mark six rectangles 2½ in. (6.5 cm) wide and approximately 8½ in. (14 cm) long (or the measurement around your napkin roll plus 3 in. [7.6 cm] for button overlap). Draw curve at both ends. Cut out napkin rings.

3. Make covered buttonhole.

Cut square of fabric for covered buttonhole 2½ by 1¾ in. (6.5 x 4.5 cm).

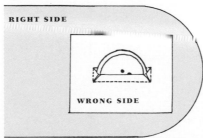

Place on one curved end of napkin ring, right sides facing. Mark rectangle diameter of button. Proceed as for covered buttonhole as described in chapter 8.

4. Add welt.

Make welt if needed (see instructions in chapter 2). Starting at opposite end from buttonhole, sew welt to edge of napkin ring using zipper foot to get close to cord. Clip welt around curves. Finish ends of welt as in chapter 2.

5. Add back.

With right sides facing, sew welted front to back of napkin ring, using previous stitches as guide. Turn right side out through buttonhole.

6. Finishing.

Hand hem back of buttonhole. Sew button in place. Press and button ring onto napkin. Repeat with other five.

Summer Napkins and Napkin Rings

NAPKINS

A classic chintz, inspired by the shapes of coral, is used to make a table mat padded with flannel, backed with solid polished cotton, and welted with colors picked out from the print.

Those who like to give elegant dinner parties frequently strive to produce different attractive, or even spectacular, decorations. Frequent galas may require several sets of tablecloths and napkins for variety. Solid-color floor-length tablecloths can be dressed up with more elaborate over-cloths, such as "theme" prints, sparkling lamé, or frothy eyelet overlays, all of which can be made at home.

Mats were originally put on a tablecloth to designate the most illustrious person at the table. Place mats on bare tables came into general use in the twentieth century and were at first considered very modern, even a bit flashy. Now we use place mats more frequently than tablecloths because they re-

Place Mats with Double Welt

A double layer of cotton flannel is enclosed between the front and the back of the place mat to help protect the table. If you choose, you can topstitch the front of the mat to the flannel in a diamond or checked design to give the effect of quilting. For this project the more expensive fabric is used for the front of the mat, and the back can be made from one of the welt fabrics — which can also be used to make simple coordinating napkins.

Six place mats 16 by 12 inches (41.7 x 30.5 cm) can be cut from ¾ yard (68.7 cm) of 54-inch (1.37 m) wide fabric if the design is of an overall type. More yardage is needed if mats have to be spaced around a larger print design. Place mats can be made smaller if desired. Yardage given here is for six mats.

Materials
- ¾ yd. (68.7 cm) of 54-in. (1.37 m) fabric for front of 6 mats
- 1½ yd. (1.37 m) polished cotton for first welt and back
- ¾ yd. (68.7 cm) polished cotton for second welt
- 1½ yd. (1.37 cm) of 54-in. (1.37 m) cotton flannel
- 18 yd. (16.45 m) welting cord filler ³⁄₁₆ in. (5 mm) in diameter

You Will Also Need
Yardstick or right-angled ruler, marking pencil, scissors, sewing machine with zipper foot, matching threads, sewing needle, iron and ironing board

1. Cut front of mat.
Select placement of fabric design on mat. On flat space, lay fabric for front of mat, right side facing down (if print design is still discernable). Mark, then cut six identical rectangles 13 by 17 in. (33 x 43 cm).

2. Cut flannel.
Cut similar rectangles in doubled-up flannel.

3. Sew front to flannel.
Lay front fabric onto double flannel and machine baste (use big stitch) around edge.

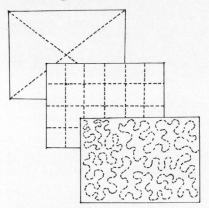

Add quilted effect, such as diagonals, checks, or freehand "vermicelli," if desired.

4. Cut back of mat.
Cut identical rectangles in your choice of backing.

5. Cut welting.
From cotton fabric for first welt, cut strips on the true bias 1½ in. (4 cm) wide and join each segment into single strip approximately 9 yd. (8.23 m) long. From second color, cut bias strips 2 in. (5.1 cm) wide and join into one strip. Press seams open.

6. Trap cord in welt fabric.
Attach zipper foot. Lay cord in center of bias strip, then fold bias over cord so it is covered, with raw edges together (see instructions in chapter 2). Stitch close to enclosed cord. Complete with both colors of fabric.

Lay narrower welt close up to wider welt and stitch the two together. Trim raw edges to an even ½ in. (12.7 mm) seam allowance.

7. Attach welt to mat front.
If mat design has a one-way direction, start at the center bottom by making notch there. Lay double welt at notch, right sides facing. Allow extra inch of welt before starting to sew and after returning to starting point for seaming welts. Use zipper foot to sew welt to mat, taking ½ in. (12.7 mm) seam allowance. Use previous stitching as a guide. Notch welt at corners. For a perfect finish, seam each color of welt separately at center bottom.

8. Assemble mat.
On flat space, lay front of mat right side up. Lay back of mat on top, right side facing down. Pin together. Stitch all layers together, pushing welts to left of needle. Use zipper foot to get as close to welt as possible. Use previous stitching (on flannel side) as guide.

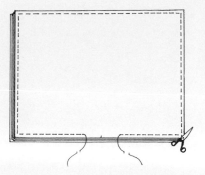

Leave space for turning. Trim seams to ¼ in. (6.4 mm) and clip corners.

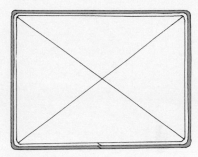

9. Finishing.
Turn right side out. Slip-stitch opening. Press. Repeat with rest of mats.

Sewing Tip
You can give a quilted effect that outlines the printed design on the front of mat. To do this, before cutting exact size of place mats, place fabric and flannel in an embroidery frame. Remove machine foot. Machine stitch in freehand style following printed design, then cut accurate rectangles.

MATS *Place Mats with Double Welt*

quire less upkeep. Individual mats may be added on top of a tablecloth to make a decorative statement.

Creating place mats from fabric of your choice is not difficult. You may wish to use a fabric that goes well with your tableware. Commercially produced mats are often printed with a border. For the preceding project, the double welt trimming—of solid cotton—is added to help tie together the colors in the print and "fence in" the mat with a created border. You can make a single welt if you prefer, in which case, the mat will be reversible.

Table runners were first used to cover temporary side "boards," then to protect the surfaces of permanent sideboards and dressers. Now a fancy runner is often laid down the middle of a dining table purely as decoration. (See the photographs opposite and on the next page.)

When you make your own table runners, you can pick luxurious fabrics and make the runners reversible to reflect the changes of season. The one pictured here is made of a red Indian silk woven with gold; on the reverse is a pink, green, and ivory taffeta stripe. Because the ivory is light colored, interfacing was sewn between the two fabrics so the red would not show through. If the fabric you select is light colored in places, interface with firm sheeting, which will also add body. Other suitable table

This reversible table runner—the top being of Indian silk mixed with gold thread—is trimmed at either end with a painted wooden bell. The runner reverses to a lighter, more summery color, which can be seen in the next photograph. The six-inch-square napkins are also of Indian silk, the green ones trimmed at the corners with diminutive handmade tassels made from sewing threads, and the red ones with tiny gold-ball buttons.

Table Runner

This runner should be dry-cleaned unless you are a very skilled hand launderer, and the bells should be removed for either process.

Materials
- Fabric the length of table, plus 12 in. (30.5 cm) for overhang, by 8 to 12 in. (20.5 to 30.5 cm) wide
- Complementary fabric, same amount, for reverse side
- Interfacing fabric, same amount, if needed
- 2 wooden bells or 2 complementary tassels
- Acrylic paints, water, paint rag, fine watercolor brush, clear acrylic coating for bells

You Will Also Need
Sewing machine, matching thread, yardstick, pencil, iron and ironing board, sewing needle, pins

1. Cut runner.
On large flat surface, cut strip of runner fabric, down grain, in width you have selected plus ½ in. (1.3 cm) on either side.

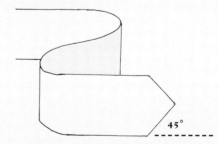

At either end of runner, cut point at 45-degree angle. Using this as pattern, cut identical piece in complementary fabric. Cut interfacing if needed.

2. Sew runner.
Lay both runner fabrics together, right sides facing. Lay on top of interfacing, if needed, with lighter fabric next to interfacing. Pin all three pieces together. Taking ½-in. (1.3 cm) seams, sew all around runner, leaving 9-in. (23 cm) gap for turning on one side. Trim point. Turn right side out and press. Slip-stitch opening.

3. Paint and attach bells.
Assemble acrylic paints, water, and fine watercolor brush. On scrap paper, try out scheme for stripes. When satisfied, draw width of each stripe around middle of each bell with pencil, making sure stripe arrangement fits bell size. You may have to make several attempts before you get it perfect. Decide colors for inside of bell, clapper, knob on top, and rim at bottom of bell. Be prepared to mix several paints to achieve ideal colors. With red, blue, yellow, black, and white, almost any color can be mixed.

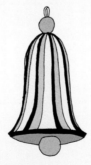

Stripes will diminish toward top of bell and widen toward bottom. Mix first stripe color and paint each stripe on both bells. Proceed with second and third colors. Acrylic paint dries quickly, so you can overlap one color on next to correct wobbly stripes. Paint inside of bells. Paint clappers. Paint knobs. Finally, paint rims, which look best in a strong, dark color. When paint is completely dry, spray with fixative, following directions on can. Spray in several separate sessions, letting each coat dry and turning bells so as to coat all sides. Sew bells onto ends of runner.

The reverse side of the runner seen in the previous photo-graph is used for setting up a summer buffet.

width of the stripe on the lighter colored side. To save fabric, you can make seams across the runner, but incorporate them into the design, by changing the direction of the fabric, for instance, or putting welting between each seam.

To embellish the ends, cut each one to a point and hang a tassel. Passementerie tassels can be found in stores that specialize in decorative trim-mings. Look for the kind of tassels that are often hung on the keys of antique bureaus. Another kind of trimming—as shown in the photograph—is a bell made of wood, painted in stripes to coordinate with the fabric. Woodcrafters make these, or you can get them at craft stores. The bell shown is painted in red, green, and yellow stripes, with the clapper and knob of gold. Use acrylic paint and spray with glossy clear acrylic fixative to give the bell a slight shine. Alternatively, buy cedar acorns and simply attach an eyelet screw.

For a special occasion, it is a nice idea to coordi-nate the buffet or hors d'oeuvres table by having fes-tive cocktail napkins designed to blend with a cen-tral table runner. The ones shown are made of Indian silk plaid.

Cocktail napkins may be twelve inches square if they are to be used for serious hors d'oeuvres, or they can be as small as six-inch squares, as are the cocktail napkins shown here.

These napkins have simple machine-stitched hems, but at each corner a novel embellishment is added. One idea, described below, is to make tiny tassels out of ordinary sewing thread selected in complementary colors. Another is to sew tiny gold ball-shaped buttons with shanks on each corner. You could add several beads in coordinated colors, or any number of other items.

runner fabrics include velvet, damask, and printed linen with an appropriate design. If no fabrics are available in the colors you want, consider getting wide grosgrain ribbon and applying strips of nar-rower ribbon onto it for color.

Cut the length of the runner to complement your table; establish the width according to the design of the selected fabric. The design should be centered on the runner, which can range from 8 to 12 inches (20.5 to 30.5 cm) wide. The finished width of the one pictured is 10 inches (25.5 cm) because that is the

Cocktail Napkins

These napkins are best washed in cool water by hand.

Materials
- ½ yd. (23 cm) of 45-in. (1.15 m) fabric (for 8 to 10 napkins)
- 24 gold-ball buttons with shanks

You Will Also Need
Sewing machine, matching thread for hemming and two other coordinating threads for tassels, scissors, ruler, pencil, iron and ironing board, sewing needle

1. Cut napkins.
Press fabric to remove wrinkles. Establish exact horizontal grain. Examine design on fabric and select center of napkins. Mark 8-in. (20.5 cm) squares on fabric and cut.

2. Sew napkins.
Press ⅛ in. (3 mm) then ¼ in. (6 mm) hem all around napkins. With a small stitch and number 11 needle, machine topstitch hems, keeping them as dainty as possible. Press napkins.

3. Make tassels.
Select three sewing threads to complement napkin fabric — one should be thread used for hemming. With one thread on top spindle of sewing machine, one on threading spindle, and the third in your lap, take all three threads and wind them loosely over your first three fingers 35 times.

Remove from fingers. Bend circle of thread flat and wind a separate thread several times over the middle and tie tightly.

Bend threads in two, with tied threads at top. Wind a separate thread 8 times around ⅛ in. (3 mm) below tie to form a "head" and tie off.

Cut through the thread loops and snip tassel "skirt" to desired length. Overall length of tassels pictured is ⅞ in. (3.3 cm).

By hand, sew tassels or buttons to corners of each napkin.

The fabric you use can be scraps; indeed, every napkin might be a different fabric. Only small pieces are needed because each napkin measures only seven or eight inches square. You can get five napkins out of one-quarter yard (23 cm) of 45-inch (1.15 m) wide fabric. The Indian silk used here was chosen to complement a dining room with red-and-green wallpaper. Both the predominantly red-colored and green-colored silk had noticeable plaid designs, so I cut each napkin exactly the same, centering the plaids and using the design to dictate the size.

Festive occasions always need special linens. For Christmas and Thanksgiving we often use a white damask, lace, or embroidered tablecloth. My favorite is a heavy linen cloth with fancy hemstitching that could almost be used as a bedspread; another is an Irish custom-embroidered linen cloth with matching napkins that was made to the dimensions of our oval table. When I was a child, for parties my mother would lay a tablecloth on the floor and surround it with cushions for us to sit on, as there were always too many for the table. I hope my daughters will remember some of the special parties of their childhood, because I used to love making decorations for their parties. For Jassy's second birthday one June, I cut out a felt lily pad shape for everyone to sit around on the floor. My husband, Keith, was a convincing Frog Prince in a mask and elegant jacket and knee britches.

The following two projects describe how to make a simple square tablecloth and a circular table skirt. There are many variations on this theme, some of which are described below. It is an especially good idea to make a simple, unlined square tablecloth out of the same fabric as a quilted circular table skirt that reaches the floor. The unlined rectangular cloth can take the brunt of wear and be easily removed for cleaning.

The greatest difficulty in making large tablecloths is finding a large flat space upon which to cut and lay fabric. I cut large projects on the dining-room table, which is convenient because it can be walked all around. I have also had to cut fabric on the floor. Another solution is to have a couple of inexpensive metal folding tables that can be pushed together to create a fairly large flat space. Patience is also needed to match printed designs; even the smallest pattern has to be matched, as it shows so much on the top surface of a table. The time spent cutting accurately is well worthwhile. The sewing is comparatively easy.

Circular tables with floor-length skirts give an impression of luxury in many rooms. Small tables, about twenty inches in diameter, can be placed at the end of a sofa or beside a bed to hold a lamp, books, glasses, and decorative objects. It is a good idea to put a circle of beveled glass on top so the fabric will not be spoiled. A larger table, say fifty inches across, is an effective focal point in a hall or living room to hold flowers, collections of small objects, or mail and keys. A circular side table in a dining room can be used for serving or as an extra table when there is a large number of guests. The table beneath the skirt need only be rudimentary, as it does not show. The lining of the skirt will not show either and can be any fabric compatible with the outer cloth. A good choice is a glazed cotton, which is relatively inexpensive and washable, but firm and with plenty of body. Plain white or natural work with most fabrics, but you can find plenty of colors if you want the lining to match your cloth.

A simple table topped with a circle of plywood can be made to look luxurious even when not in use as a dining table if covered with a floor-length quilted circular skirt.

OPPOSITE: A breakfast table in a summer cottage is set with a cheerful cotton cloth, daisy-shaped plates, and handmade chicken egg cozies.

The amount of material needed will depend on the size of the table and the design of your fabric. If it is a print with a large design repeat, for instance, you will need extra fabric for matching at the seams. A general rule for calculating the length of fabric to buy for a small repeat is to measure the diameter of the table and add twice its height. Double that mea-surement and add a foot for seams and matching. If the table is very big across, you may need three times, rather than twice the length. Keep seam al-lowances as small as a half inch so seams curve eas-ily at the hem.

After these instructions you will find other, more complicated variations on circular table skirts.

Square Tablecloth

This is a simple project that rests on the choice of fabric. If the table is large, the cloth will have to be seamed, and these seams have to match. A general rule is never to have a seam right in the center of a tablecloth unless it is part of the design (as, for instance, in the mitered striped tablecloth in the photograph on page 61). Instead, center the fabric on the table and add pieces on the sides, where the seams will be less obvious (see illustration opposite).

Dry-clean if the fabric is precious or if you apply trimming that may not be washable. Untrimmed cotton cloths can be washed, but carefully, and best by hand.

Fabric amounts given are for a cloth 60 in. (1.53 m) square.

Materials
• 4 yd. (4.91 m) of 45-in. (1.15 m) fabric

You Will Also Need
Yardstick, tape measure, marking pencil, cutting shears, scissors, sewing machine (with zigzag or hemming attachment optional), matching thread, iron and ironing board, sewing needle (if hand hemming)

1. Cut fabric.
Decide where design should fall on center of table. Cut length 66 in. (1.68 m) long, centered on chosen design.

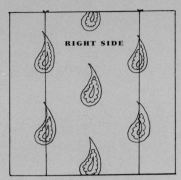

RIGHT SIDE

Cut strips 66 in. (1.68 m) long for sides, matching design of fabric at selvages, to make up 66-in. (1.68 m) width.

2. Seam cloth.
Trim off selvages. Seam cloth. Open seams and finish with a turned edge or zigzag stitch. Press seams open.

3. Sew hem.
Press up 3-in. (7.6 cm) hem on each side. Miter corners on wrong side. Hems can be finished with machine topstitching, machine felling, or by hand stitching.

Design Ideas
Add a border, as shown in the photograph on page 58.

Sewing Tips
For an outdoor tablecloth, hang tassels at corners to weight it in case the weather gets windy. You can also cover tailoring weights with matching fabric and fasten them to the wrong side of the cloth with Velcro. This way they can be removed when the cloth is cleaned. Another way to weight outdoor tablecloths is to sew a line of tailoring beads inside the hem.

Lined Circular Table Skirt

Materials
• Calculate amount of fabric needed by measuring diameter of table and adding twice its height. Double this measurement (or triple if the table is very big) and add some extra for matching if fabric has large repeat. Six yd. (5.5 m) is an average amount.
• Same amount of lining fabric, minus extra for matching

You Will Also Need
Yardstick and tape measure, marking pencil, cutting shears, sewing machine, matching thread, iron and ironing board, pins, sewing needle

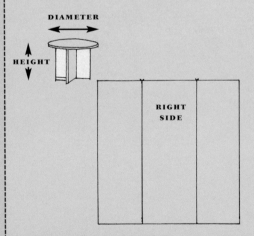

DIAMETER

HEIGHT

RIGHT SIDE

1. Cut table skirt.
If design of fabric has large repeat, select motif for center. Cut piece of fabric length of table diameter plus twice its height, adding seam allowances of ½ in. (12.7 mm).

This piece will run across center of table. Side pieces will be joined to this and must match at seams. Cut two more pieces for sides, same length as center piece, to complete overall size.

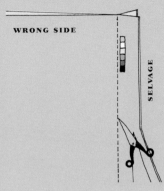

2. Sew panels.
Sew side pieces to each side of main panel, matching design at selvages. Cut away extra-wide selvages — often found in decorator fabrics — to prevent seams from pulling, especially after table skirt is dry-cleaned or washed. Press seams open.

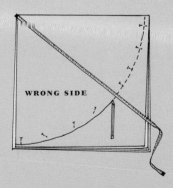

3. Cut circle.
Lay fabric right side up on large flat surface and fold in quarters so wrong side is facing out. With tape measure held at folded corner, mark

quarter-circle of desired length, as explained in step 1, with pins and then pencil.

4. Cut lining.
Cut two pieces (or more if table is extra large) same length as table skirt in lining fabric.

5. Sew lining.
Sew pieces of lining together. Leave opening of about 12 in. (30 cm) in middle of seam (or one of multiple seams) for turning later (in step 6). Press center seam (or seams) open.

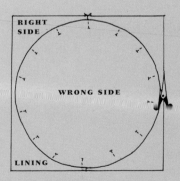

6. Cut lining circle.
On large flat space, lay outer table skirt on lining rectangle, right sides facing and grains matching. Smooth evenly and pin around edge. Use outside table skirt as pattern and cut lining into identical circle.

7. Sew table skirt to lining.
With right sides facing, sew two circles together, taking ½-in. (12.7 mm) seams. Turn inside out through opening in lining.

8. Finishing.
Press so that seam is at edge around bottom of cloth (called knife edge). If necessary, topstitch edge ¾ in. (19.1 mm) to prevent lining from showing. Slip stitch opening in lining by hand.

Sewing Tip
Never let lining be smaller than outside cloth or table skirt will always look wrinkled. If anything, veer toward having lining ¼ in. (6.4 mm) larger all around to allow for shrinkage when cleaned.

Design Variations
- Velvet with lace overskirt (see photograph of bedroom, page 132).
- Silk taffeta table skirt for stylish city living room.
- Quilted skirt, as seen in photograph on page 59.

Unlined Square Tablecloth with Border

This bordered square cloth is laid over a matching quilted circular cloth for casual dining. The sunny yellow Provençal cotton had its own border printed along one edge. The border was cut away and applied around the edge of this square cloth, with mitering at the corners. It may not be convenient to find a fabric with a border printed along the selvage. Another way to achieve this effect is to find a different but compatible fabric to use as a border. The sewing method will be the same.

Because the square cloth takes the brunt of wear, requiring frequent laundering, it is best to preshrink the fabric before cutting and stitching by running it through the hot rinse cycle of the washing machine. Iron while it is still slightly damp to remove all wrinkles.

Materials
• 16 yd. (14.24 m) of fabric for both tablecloth and quilted table skirt (14 yd. would be plenty if you are not making a border)

You Will Also Need
Yardstick, tape measure, 45-degree set square, marking pencil, cutting scissors, sewing machine, matching thread, iron and ironing board

This sunny yellow cloth, shown here on its own, was designed to be used over a matching circular quilted table skirt, seen in the next photograph.

1. Cut tablecloth.
Cut main center part of tablecloth following instructions in step 1, page 56, and adding panels on sides to get desired width. Match pattern where necessary. Allow ¾ in. (19.1 mm) seam allowances.

2. Sew side panels to center panel.
Sew panels, taking ¾-in. (19.1 mm) seam allowance, and finish seams off with fold-over topstitch. Press seams open.

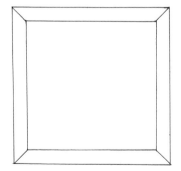

3. Cut border.
Though width of border will vary from fabric to fabric, and from table size to table size, they should all miter at the corners at 45-degree angle.

4. Apply border.
Lay border along edges of tablecloth, matching where needed so mitered seams at corners will match or look good. Pin right side of border to wrong side of cloth, matching as you go. Stitch along one side, then repeat on all sides. Press knife-edge seam.

5. Stitch miters.
Stitch miters at 45-degree angles.

6. Topstitch border.
Press ¼-in. (6.4 mm) seam allowance to wrong side on edge where border joins main part of cloth. Pin all around. Topstitch in place.

7. Finishing.
Press well.

Matching Quilted Circular Table Skirt

This circular quilted table skirt reaches the floor and can be used with the square bordered tablecloth described above overlaying it, or on its own. When used with the square cloth, this skirt can be a permanent feature in a room; the over-cloth is washable and easily removed if soiled.

For this project you will need to locate a professional quilter and send seamed fabric away to be processed. Be sure to look at all the styles of quilting available and pick the stitch best suited to your fabric. The stitch shown is a vermicelli pattern.

To calculate how much fabric you will need for the quilted table skirt, measure as for a plain circular skirt (see page 56) but add 10 inches (25.5 cm) in both directions to allow for quilting. The cloth shown on this page is for a table 48 inches (1.22 m) in diameter and 30 inches (76.2 cm) high. This size table can seat four to six people.

The lining can be made of any plain cotton, as it will not show. White and natural are usually the least expensive.

Materials
- 7 yd. (6.40 m) of 50-in. (1.27 m) wide fabric
- 6½ yd. (5.94 m) of plain 50-in. (1.27 m) wide lining

You Will Also Need
Yardstick, tape measure, 45-degree set square, marking pencil, cutting scissors, sewing machine, matching thread, iron and ironing board, access to professional quilter

This yellow quilted table skirt was designed to be used in conjunction with the square yellow bordered cloth.

1. Cut and sew fabric for quilting.
Join printed fabric into square 10 in. (25.5 cm) longer and wider than needed for circular table skirt. As described on page 57, do not join panels with seam down center but instead add fabric to sides of center panel, matching seams. Press seams open. Send to quilter and select type of quilting desired.

2. Cut circle.
When quilting is completed, cut quilted fabric into circle of desired size following instructions in step 1, page 56.

3. Cut lining.
In plain cloth, cut lining fabric same size as quilted circle. Lining can have center seam. Leave gap in center of seam for turning fabrics right side out after stitching. Press seam open.

4. Join quilting and lining.
Pin quilted fabric and lining together on same grains, right sides facing. Stitch together on wrong side, taking ½-in. (12.7 mm) seams. Turn right side out.

5. Finishing.
Slip-stitch gap in lining seam by hand. Press edges of table skirt lightly if needed. Topstitch through and through 1 in. (2.3 cm) from edge to prevent lining from showing.

Mitered Striped Table Skirt

This project is a variation on a simple circular table skirt. The circle is divided into quarters. Stripes are centered on each quarter and carefully matched as they are seamed together so that they form a design in the center of the table.

Buy a stripe that is balanced—that is, it looks the same going right to left and left to right. A simple two-color stripe such as the one shown in the photograph opposite is probably best. It need not necessarily be a heavy satin as shown; a crisp cotton would be effective and casual-looking, as well as easier to sew. The most economical type of stripe is one that is woven so that the back is identical to the front. If you use this type of stripe, you will need a quarter more yardage than for a plain table skirt. If the stripe has a definite right and wrong side, buy one half again as much yardage as for a plain skirt. (For instructions on calculating yardage for a circular table skirt, see page 56).

If you decide to use heavy satin, you will notice that it curls alarmingly as it is cut. Pressing frequently does help, but this problem persists until all the sewing is done and the seams are firmly in place. Be patient; the results are worth the slow going.

To be practical, have a circular glass top made for the table to protect the fabric if it is likely to get a lot of use.

For a large table, extra fabric will have to be sewn around the outer edges in order to complete the circle. These additions must match at the seams and should be sewn along the edge of a stripe to disguise the seam as much as possible. For smaller side tables in a living room, these additions may not be necessary.

For this project, accurate cutting is essential. All the striped sections must be cut with their apexes at an exact 90-degree angle—which will be at a 45-degree angle from the selvage—in order to match. Pin all seams before stitching and check each seam for matching as it is stitched and before pressing open.

Materials
- 7½ yd. (6.90 m) of 50- to 60-in. (1.27 to 1.53 m) wide fabric (for a table 48 inches [1.22 m] in diameter)
- 6½ yd. (5.95 m) of 54-in. (1.37 m) wide cotton lining

You Will Also Need
Sewing machine with zipper foot, matching thread, scissors, marking pencil, yardstick, tape measure, set square or right-angled ruler, sewing needle, iron and ironing board

1. Cut table skirt.
Measure across top of table; divide measurement in half to get radius. Measure table height. Add radius to height to get length of each quarter of circular skirt. With right-angled ruler or set square, mark 90-degree angle on bias in center of stripe chosen for center of table skirt.

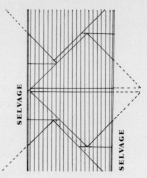

Draw extended bias lines to selvages. Add width if needed to complete triangle that will be cut into quarter circles. Pin these extensions on, carefully matching stripes. Add seam allowances. Mark into quarter circles and cut, complete with necessary extensions.

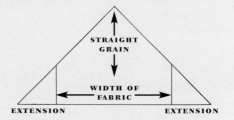

2. Sew on extensions (if needed).
Sew extensions on to complete each quarter if necessary, matching along edges of stripes exactly to disguise seams. Press seams open.

3. Sew two quarters.
Sew two completed quarters together to form a half circle, pinning stripes so they match before sewing. After sewing, check carefully and make any necessary adjustments so that each strip miters perfectly. Press open. Sew other two quarters in similar manner.

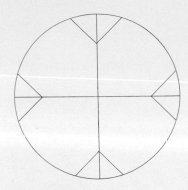

4. Join halves.

Pin two halves together to form circle, matching carefully and adjusting where necessary. Sew, check, and cut away any excess seam turnings. Press open.

5. Sew lining.

Lining can have one central seam, as it will not show. Cut two pieces the diameter of table skirt and sew together at selvages, leaving a 12-in. (30 cm) gap in center of seam for turning. If table is large, three lengths may be needed. Gap can be in either seam. Press seam or seams open. Cut to circle shape by placing table skirt on top of seamed piece of lining and using it as a pattern.

6. Assemble skirt.

On flat space, lay lining and mitered table skirt right sides facing, matching grain. Sew around edge. Remove any loose threads, as these will show through on right side if they are trapped inside. Pull tablecloth right side out through opening. Slip-stitch lining opening by hand.

7. Finishing.

Press table skirt. A topstitch can be added if desired, but with a luxurious fabric like heavy satin, a topstitch may cheapen the effect.

Design Ideas

- Use lighter stripe in pattern (if there is one) for center of table, otherwise design may look like an iron cross in the center.
- A variation might be to add a padded border and a multicolored cord, as in the photograph. You will need a roll of flat batting used for making quilts, which can be cut to curved shape, and 9½-yd. (8.70 m) cording.
- If inserting cording on tape at bottom of hem, measure tape on cording and make seams same width.

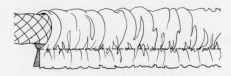

- A ¾-in. (19.1 mm) wide gathered welting can be added at the hem to give a nice finish. This will take another ¾ yd. (68.5 cm) of fabric for bias strips, plus 10 yd. (9.14 m) of ¾-in. (19.1 mm) welting filler. (A gathered welt is made the same way as a smooth welt except that the fabric is pushed into gathers and the welting cord is pulled while stitching.)

A yellow-and-white-striped and mitered table skirt disguises a plain plywood circular table in a large drawing room.

Sewing Tip

Table skirts can be made with both a wide gathered welt and an inserted cord, but this requires size 16 or 18 needle, as many layers get very thick and break regular needles.

Kitchens, Pantries, and Laundries

WORK ROOMS

BEHIND THE FRONT ROOMS IN every household are the rooms where many of us spend most of our time — the work rooms. In larger houses, families tend to gather in the kitchen. In apartments, unless one is very lucky, kitchens tend to be small, but large or small, kitchens need to be supplied with linens in the form of dish towels, hand towels, and oven cloths.

Kitchen linens might also include informal napkins and casual tablecloths, tray cloths, and place mats, as well as polishing cloths, aprons, and unessential but charming oddments like tea and egg cozies.

Dish towels come in many varieties. They are still particularly useful in the kitchen despite our reliance on dishwashers to do most of the drying automatically. We tend to accumulate dish towels (known variously as drying cloths, glass cloths, and tea towels), because they have become, along with theme mugs, one of the prime souvenir items in most museum and country house gift shops.

Printed linen dish towels usually have such a glossy finish when new that they are almost useless. They become softer and more absorbent when broken in with use, but you have to accept that the printed design then becomes blurred and faded.

Table linens are stored in this high breakfast-room wall closet for use in the kitchen and dining room.

PREVIOUS PAGES:
LEFT: *In the early 1930s, a washed and bleached twenty-five-pound sugar bag was used to make a pretty drying cloth by Mary Lee Rogers, who appliquéd onto it, with tiny hand-hemming stitches, a cotton fabric printed with fruit.*
RIGHT: *Vintage drying cloths depict lovebirds performing different household chores for each day of the week. Patterns for this type of embroidery were found in five-and-dime stores and ironed onto fabric.*

There is a certain charm to this faded look, especially when you know that a faded towel will dry dishes far more efficiently.

An associate of my husband's collects kitchen linens from the 1920s. These are naively embroidered in simple stitches that were once colorful but have now taken on a period pallor. She gave us a set of deliciously softened vintage towels, embroidered for each day of the week. Lovebirds with appliquéd wings are depicted doing different daily household chores: hanging washing on the line on Monday, ironing on Tuesday, and so on.

Dish towels were once made from old flour sacks or even from sugar bags (which were finer cotton). Many farm families made clothing from flour sacks, especially for children. Fashion designer Leamond Dean tells how his mother made his first underwear from flour sacks, bleached to remove the labeling and complete with hand-sewn buttonholes. He gave me the dish towel in the photograph on page 62, which was made by his great-aunt Lee from a twenty-five-pound sugar bag.

The late art consultant Wade McCann proudly displayed in his Greenwich Village apartment crammed with glass and china antiques a flour-bag tablecloth embroidered by his Texas grandfather with drawn-thread work. The ghost of the flour-sack label still showed. Very few antique kitchen towels have survived, because they are always well used and worn out, as is Ella Kruger's embroidered poem on page 22.

Because linen is so absorbent, it makes wonderfully smooth drying towels. They can be found in traditional windowpane checks, or printed as souvenirs of famous places or in any number of designs. They can be made in smooth linen weaves or in thick, porous cotton honeycomb and huckaback weaves. Ladies also used to knit dishcloths in heavy, soft natural-colored string.

Tray cloths were a mainstay of the linen drawer in times gone by. They were used on breakfast trays, such as the one in the photograph on page 132, on tea trays and butler's trays for drinks, and on trinket trays such as that on page 79. They are no longer the essential part of a household they once were, but they do add a nice touch. Another use for them, as for doilies, is to make them into beautiful boudoir pillows.

Drawers in a vacation cottage hold casual, colorful tablecloths, napkins, and tea towels.

In this farmhouse kitchen, the simple table is covered with a hand-stitched cloth that was pieced from scraps, as was the patchwork rug.

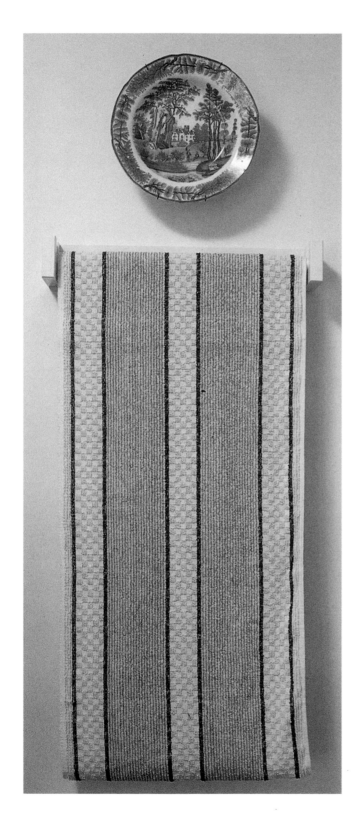

Drying cloths are stacked in a glass-fronted kitchen cupboard.

Every well-equipped kitchen used to have a towel on a roller for drying hands. This one came in a set of three: blue, green, and red with natural coloring, complete with a wooden roller.

This apron, made by fashion designer Meredith Gladstone, is perfect for a hostess to wear over a long skirt. The waistband is a headband from a sailor's hat, and insignia from nautical uniforms have been appliquéd. Tricolored herringbone stitch outlines the sides.

On this weathered bench is a baby's bib made from a Provençal print.

Aprons of all kinds are stored in kitchen closets and drawers. They may be made of a simple cotton print, or a spongeable vinyl-coated fabric, or even, as above, of silk to be worn over a long skirt. Aprons make great gifts. A friend of ours had a business custom-making aprons for special occasions and as gifts. There was a time that no one did any work in the kitchen without putting on an apron, but times and technologies have changed, and now our clothes are as easy to launder as aprons are.

If you have a baby in the family, a stock of baby's bibs is a necessary addition to the linen drawer. As parents of infants know, there are never enough bibs. They wear out quickly because they get very

Baby's Bib

Materials
- Fabric 9 by 20 in. (23 x 51 cm)
- ½ yd. (46 cm) narrow ribbon for ties (optional)

You Will Also Need
Firm paper to make pattern, marking pencil, scissors, sewing machine, matching thread, sewing needle, iron and ironing board

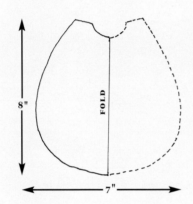

1. Make pattern.
On paper, draw shape as in illustration. Measurements indicated allow for ¼-in. (6.4 mm) seam allowance. Fold pattern through center to make sure both sides are same shape and to establish vertical grain line.

2. Cut bib.
On wrong side of fabric, place paper pattern, centering on chosen design. Trace pattern. Repeat for back of bib. Cut. Cut two strips 1¼ by 9 in. (3.3 x 23 cm) for self ties (not needed if you use ribbon ties).

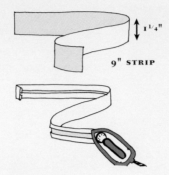

9" STRIP

3. Sew ties.
Press ¼-in. (6.4 mm) fold down each side and one end of each tie.

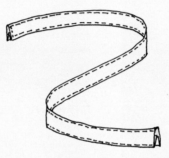

Press in half lengthwise. Edge-stitch around ties.

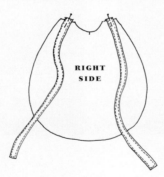

RIGHT SIDE

4. Sew bib.
Pin ties to either side of shoulders on right side of front of bib, raw edges together, with ties hanging toward body of bib.

A clown doll sits in the sunlight wearing a bib made from a Provençal print.

WRONG SIDE

Lay back side of bib on top, right sides facing. Starting ½ in. (12.7 mm) in on one side of neckline, sew all around bib to a similar point on other side of neckline, leaving opening in the middle. Catch ties on shoulders as you sew. Be careful not to catch ties in rest of bib seam.

5. Finishing.
Trim and clip seams. Turn bib right side out through neck opening. Slip-stitch neck opening by hand. If desired, edge-stitch all around bib, catching opening at neck as you stitch. Press bib.

BIB *Baby's Bib*

stained. But the good news is that bibs are easy to make and use hardly any fabric, so they can be made from scraps.

When choosing fabric for bibs, remember that patterned cloth does not show stains as easily as plain. It is amusing to use unexpected fabrics — a sophisticated chintz, an ocelot print, or a stylish toile, for instance — so long as the fabric you select is washable and soft enough for a baby. The ties can be made from narrow ribbon or from self fabric. Use the selvage for ties if it is interesting. The sides can be different to make a reversible bib. In the photograph on page 67, a baby's bib was made to match the napkins used by the grown-ups.

Shapes of bibs can vary. The instructions here are for the simplest and smallest variety, perfect for a newborn. It has a curved shape, with ties at the neck. Bibs can be square shaped or have pockets across the bottom, useful for catching bits when baby gets older and starts trying to feed him- or herself. Larger bibs are needed, of course, as baby grows.

Bibs can have appliquéd designs, or embroidered initials, or be made to match a special outfit. There are endless variations on this basic recipe for a bib. The fabric you use will suggest ideas.

As bibs are so quick and easy to make, you can give sets of three or more as a shower gift. It is a good idea, therefore, to make a firm paper pattern that you can use many times over.

Pot holders can be bought at kitchenware and gift shops in many varieties, from plain to fancy. I always liked the simple tabby-weave ones my children made in school. Pot holders can be made from leftover scraps of quilting or from fabric with batting or layers of flannel trapped between and machine quilted together. Choose simple but unexpected shapes, such as triangles, stars, and octagons, as well as the usual circles and squares. It is fun to use the same fabric as kitchen curtains or cushions and bind the edges with contrasting or self fabric.

It is very English to use tea cozies; probably because more tea is drunk in England and houses are often much colder than in the United States. We have quite a collection of tea cozies — some from the past and others that friends have given us thinking that without them we cannot exist. They are not used all the time, but my husband, Keith, tends to use them because he likes tea strong and hot. Like tea towels, tea cozies tend to come as whimsical, kitschy souvenirs. We were just given one that depicts Queen Elizabeth I. Our most useful tea cozy is also the most worn out. It is hideous, but it fits almost every teapot, however unlikely the shape. Another is made of silk satin with colorful Indian embroidery and shaped a bit like a bishop's miter.

The tea cozy pictured on page 70 was made from a scrap of red-and-white reversible matelassé fabric. The cat design seemed to lend itself to a domed shape, and the fabric already had a padded effect, so it was perfect. Choose any type of fabric that strikes your fancy, thick or thin. If it is thin, add several layers of batting. The lining can contrast or be just plain sheeting. For this cozy I used a scrap of red herringbone cotton as a lining.

There are many designs of tea cozies, some with openings for the teapot handle and spout. The one shown is the simplest variety, a curved dome that will fit on many types of teapots.

The butler's pantry is a service room between the kitchen and dining room that was once the domain of the butler, who, together with the housekeeper, ran the household for large well-to-do families. The

Tea Cozy

Materials

- Scrap of suitable material about 12 by 30 in. (31 by 77 cm)
- Similar amount of fabric for lining
- ½ yd. (46 cm) of batting, such as fiberfill or cotton batting in sheets

You Will Also Need

Marking pencil, scissors, sewing machine, matching thread, sewing needle

1. Cut outside cozy.

Taking into account design of outside fabric and size of teapot, cut dome-shaped pattern in brown paper. Add ½ in. (12.7 mm) for seams all around. Lay pattern on fabric, paying attention to placement on design. Mark and cut two pieces.

2. Cut lining.

Cut two pieces same shape in lining fabric.

3. Cut batting.

Cut four pieces same shape in batting.

4. Cut loop.

Cut from extra piece of either outer or lining fabric a piece 4 by 1½ in. (10 x 4 cm) for hanging loop.

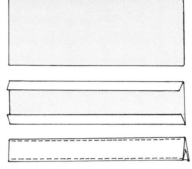

5. Make loop.

Fold ¼ in. (6.4 mm) in on long sides of loop piece. Fold in half lengthwise. Topstitch both edges.

6. Sew outside fabric.

Place outside pieces together with right sides facing. Bend loop in two and trap it between pieces at top center, with raw edges of cozy and loop ends lined up. Sew curved edges of outer pieces together, taking ½-in. (12.7 mm) seams.

7. Add batting.

Lay a double layer of batting onto each lining piece. Sew batting to lining, taking ¼ in. (6.4 mm) seam allowance. Sew lining pieces together, right sides facing, batting on outside, taking ½-in. (12.7 mm) seam allowance. Leave 4-in. (10.3 cm) gap in middle of arch for turning.

WRONG SIDE

8. Assemble cozy.
With right sides of lining and outer fabric pieces facing, sew around bottom of cozy on wrong side, taking ½-in. (12.7 mm) seams. Turn cozy right side out by pulling through gap in lining. Slip-stitch gap together by hand or simply machine-stitch edges together, as seam will not show inside cozy. Straighten cozy but do not press, as cozy should retain its puffy look.

Design Idea
Using the same principle but on a much smaller scale, make padded egg cozies.

OPPOSITE: *This tea cozy was designed around a pretty and reversible decorative fabric.*

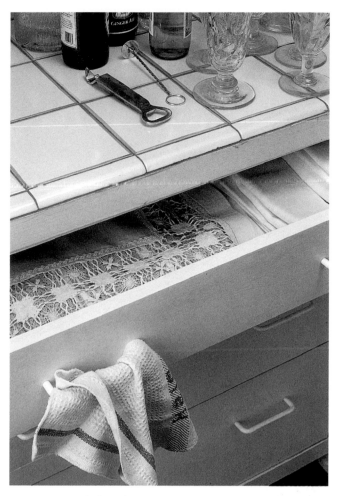

Roomy, easy-sliding drawers hold tablecloths, mats, and napkins in this passageway turned into a butler's pantry.

modern butler's pantry is a useful room where dishes, cutlery, glasses, and linens, as well as condiments and drinks, may be stored. Cupboards may contain dishes packed in zippered containers— with felt or fabric between each piece if they are antique and only used for best occasions. Cutlery may be kept in green baize–lined trays or baskets, in fabric-lined wooden boxes, or in cutlery sacks that are rolled and tied. Keeping table silver covered lessens the need for constant polishing, a chore that was always done by the butler. Nowadays, the housekeeper, male or female, has a career in addition to

maintaining the house, so cutlery that doesn't require polishing is frequently used. To keep knives, forks, and spoons in order, however, it is a nice idea to make pretty cutlery sacks or to put cutlery in wicker baskets lined with fabric that coordinates with the pantry.

The laundry room is another work room with its own set of linens. In old houses, there would always be one or often two large sinks and a huge boiler for boiling the linens on Mondays, the traditional wash day. A wringer — sometimes called a mangle — was used to squeeze out most of the water before clothes were hung outside on the line. Overhead wooden racks that let down on a pulley system were used for indoor drying.

There is still an enormous pleasure to be had in hanging washing on the line. Some people complain that fabrics are stiff when line dried, but it is that crispness, and the fresh garden smell, that I most appreciate about clothing and linens dried outdoors.

The modern utility room is much smaller than the large traditional laundry room with its deep stone sinks. A contemporary laundry may not have room for much more than a washing machine, dryer, and perhaps some shelves for cleaning items or drawers for dusters, polishing cloths, and cleanup rags. There may be a wall rack for mops and brooms, a vacuum, possibly a toolbox and step ladder, and an iron and ironing board.

Laundry bags and clothes hampers are useful accessories in a utility room. A collector I know has a series of vintage laundry bags, embroidered in the 1920s in simple surface stitches, hung on the walls of a laundry room as decoration. Everyone needs

Nightgowns hung out on the line on a sunny day.

This laundry room, between the kitchen and bathroom in a Catskills farmhouse, has a huge double sink that was installed in the early twentieth century.

A combination of cotton prints and weaves with neutral coloring are used for subtly personalized laundry bags and a matching ironing board cover.

laundry bags for home and travel. They are simple to make and, when personalized, make unusual gifts.

There are many laundry caddies set on metal and wood frames to be found in catalogs and department stores. You have to assemble the framework of the caddy yourself and attach a set of wheels. The fabric hampers slung onto these frames are usually in practical white or pastel-colored cotton or nylon, but many people prefer a laundry caddy that coordinates with their decor. It is a simple matter to copy the fabric part in your own choice of fabric. Fabric hampers are usually sewn in a rudimentary way, using large stitches and as few seams as possible.

Laundry Caddy

The laundry caddy pictured opposite is in a black, red, and white cotton tattersall check, chosen because it went with the red-and-black carpet and black, red, and white wallpaper in the bathroom. Utilizing the straight lines of the check made it easy to cut, but with a fabric like this, it is important to match the checks along the side seams and where the pocket is added. The rectangular piece at the bottom of the caddy does not show, so it does not need to match.

A hamper of this type is held in place on the frame by four loops set into the fabric base that slot onto the bars of the frame. On one side, the bars hold wheels so the caddy is mobile. The hamper is held up vertically by four wider loops set into the hem at the top. The hem is then folded over the top of the frame and held in place by tension.

Materials
- Laundry caddy frame and fabric hamper
- 1½ yd. (1.40 m) of 45- to 50-in (1.15 to 1.37 m) wide fabric

You Will Also Need
Tape measure, yardstick, marking pencil, scissors, sewing machine (preferably with zigzag attachment), matching thread, iron and ironing board, brown paper for pattern (optional)

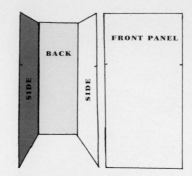

1. Cut body of hamper.
Remove original fabric hamper from caddy. Measure width of original hamper. Add seam and hem allowances. Commercial hampers are usually made of extra-wide goods and cut all in one piece. Cut your hamper instead with an extra panel. Pocket will be trapped in seams of this panel. Measure height of original hamper. Add bottom seam and top hem allowances. Make brown paper pattern if needed. Cut sides of hamper, matching design at seams. Measure base of original hamper. Add seam allowances. (This does not have to match as it will not show.) Cut base of hamper.

2. Cut and sew pocket.
If original hamper has pocket — most of them do, for tucking in small items — measure this, add seam allowance, and hem allowance for top. Cut pocket, matching to extra panel. Press ½ in. (12.7 mm) twice at hem of pocket and topstitch.

3. Attach pocket.
Pin pocket in place on side panel of hamper. Sew along raw edges to hold in place until caught in seams.

4. Make bottom loops.
Cut four pieces 4 in. (10.3 cm) square. Fold one in half, right sides facing. Sew along raw edges. Press open seam. Turn to right side. Press, centering seam. Repeat with other three.

5. Make top loops.
Cut four pieces 9 by 6 in. (23 x 15.2 cm). Fold one in half lengthwise, right sides facing. Sew along raw edges. Press open seam. Turn right side out. Press, centering seam. Repeat with other three.

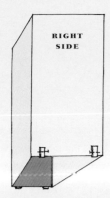

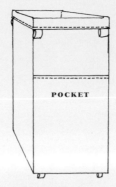

6. Place narrow loops on bottom of hamper.
Pin smaller loops in place on corners of narrower sides of bottom panel of hamper. Sew in place ready for seaming.

7. Sew side seams of hamper.
Sew vertical side seams of hamper, matching design and catching pocket in seams. To make hamper washable, seams must be finished. If sewing machine has zigzag attachment, use this to finish raw seams. If not, press seams open and topstitch each separately.

8. Add bottom of hamper.
Sew base of hamper in place, pinning first to ensure fit. Finish off seam inside with zigzag stitch (or machine stitch all seam allowances together, then pink).

9. Add top loops.
Press ½ in. (12.7 mm) twice for hem across top of hamper. Sew, tucking four large loops into hem at each corner on narrowest sides.

10. Finishing.
Press hamper. Assemble hamper on frame as original. Reattach wheels. Fold deep hem over top of frame. Secure if needed with hand tacks.

To coordinate a laundry caddy to a bathroom scheme, buy a caddy frame and use the fabric hamper that comes with it as a pattern. Here a cotton tattersall check is used to complement the red-and-black carpet and the red, white, and black wallpaper.

Bedrooms,
Dressing Rooms,
and Bathrooms

UPSTAIRS

O F ALL the rooms in the house, the most elegant linen is found in the bedroom. Sheets with richly embroidered edges and monograms, pillowcases trimmed with lace, pure silk satin bedspreads, and cashmere throws are found here. A huge armoire or deep bottom drawer, when opened, can give off the faint perfume of real lavender in sachets tucked between piles of pure linen and crisp cotton folded into neat stacks.

Fashions in decoration and in bed linens continually change, but beds have always had some sort of top covering. These covers have many different names and weights: bedspreads, coverlets, counterpanes, eiderdowns, comforters, quilts, even the Indian term *palampore* (coverlet)—the Indians having been the first to invent washable cotton fabrics. Covers may be made of a single fabric with a stitched hem at the edge or made of patchwork; they may be crocheted or knitted, and they can be lined, lined and padded, or filled with down for warmth.

Since the 1970s, the duvet—a European-style down-filled comforter—has taken over as the all-purpose coverlet in many households. Duvets are now a standard part of every linen department. A good-looking cover of washable cotton in a design and color of your choice can be easily made to disguise the plain vanilla of a standard store-bought duvet. All you do is cut and stitch a big fabric envelope the size of the duvet, complete with a fold-over flap that closes with buttons or ties.

PREVIOUS PAGES: *Complementing the exquisite scalloped-edged bed linen is a simple curtain tied back in a knot in this Kips Bay show-house room designed by Peter Carlson and Joel Gevis. (Photo by Dennis Krukowski.)*

The linen closet or a blanket chest may hold classic American blankets, such as the distinctive-looking Hudson Bay, Beacon, and blankets derived from Native American designs. Blankets range from cashmere, chenille, and mohair throws to rough army-type blankets and loose-woven cotton blankets for summer use. Quilts are often folded and stored in specially made low quilt chests or on quilt ladders, as seen on page 6.

If blankets are used rather than duvets, lightweight blanket covers are a stylish contemporary alternative to the traditional bedspread. In the eighteenth century, it was fashionable to have the bedspread, curtains, upholstery, bed hangings, and

INSET: *A dressing table is concocted by assembling lace mats and family pictures, with a tray for toiletries in the center.* BACKGROUND: *The complexity of the lace in the inset photograph can be seen in this detail and again on the endpapers of this book.*

RIGHT: *On this nineteenth-century dressing table from Maine, an heirloom linen bureau scarf is decorated with cutwork embroidery.*

OPPOSITE: *A young girl's closet is designed to hold bed linens as well as clothing.*

A seventeenth-century English mule chest is used here to store blankets. In it can be seen a cream wool Hudson Bay blanket with multicolor stripes, a dark green tartan mohair throw, a blue-and-red woven wool throw, and a red, white, and blue woven American coverlet, signed by the weaver, "B. Lighty: New Berlin." A red throw and a paisley shawl hang on the lid.

This guest-room bed in a country house is covered with a lightweight pink wool blanket on which is placed a white plissé blanket cover, letting the blanket show through. The pillow is made from bedspread fabric. The pale pink cotton voile nightgown is thickly embroidered in natural-colored thread.

The alcove bed seen on page 83 is wedged between two closets set into the eaves. In one of those closets, shown here, is stored a collection of summertime linens.

even wall covering *en suite*—all of the same fabric. The bedspread frequently is made to match the window curtains even today. Bedspreads are usually made to fold over and completely cover the bed pillows. An alternative preferred by the cosmopolitan crowd is to show one's beautiful sheets and pillowcases by using a sheer blanket cover on the bed instead of a lined bedspread.

A blanket cover is usually made of a lightweight, washable single fabric, such as piqué or, if the blanket underneath is intended to show through, something sheer or translucent, such as fine voile or batiste. Blanket covers are generally trimmed at the edges with some form of decoration, such as embroidery or bound scallops. They are easy to remove and launder, and much more convenient to deal with than heavy bedspreads. Commercial blanket covers are often made of fine nylon seersucker or cotton plissé, like that shown in the photograph on page 80.

A double bed, tucked sideways into the eaves of the summer house bedroom shown on page 83, has built-in closets on either side. A cubbyhole at the back of one of the closets functions as a night table and holds a reading light, pencil and paper, and books. A cheerfully bold linen print with chinoiserie overtones—also available at the time on a backing to use as wallpaper—was chosen to line the eaves and cover the box spring of the bed. The bedspread and fronts of the large throw pillows were made in the same fabric, but it was given dimension and body by being quilted. The quilting follows the outlines of the printed design. This type of quilting has to be sent out to be done on a professional quilting machine. The pillows are welted and backed with solid fabric—in this case, plain yellow linen.

Quilted Tuck-in Bedspread

Because the printed design used in the bedspread shown is a one-way pattern, the bedspread had to be cut following the same direction as the wall covering; in other words, sideways. The quilted bedspread tucks in under the mattress at the front, but merely hangs down the depth of the mattress on the other three sides; the front tuck-in is therefore longer. Because the quilted fabric would have made the corners too bulky to tuck, gussets of unquilted fabric were substituted at each corner. A lining of inexpensive coordinating calico print backs the bedspread, hiding the batting. The final bedspread is topstitched all around a half inch (12.7 mm) from the edges to prevent the lining from showing.

Fabric requirements are given for a double bed and four standard pillows.

Materials

- 5½ yd. (5.05 m) of 45- to 54-in. (1.15 to 1.37 m) wide bedspread fabric
- 4 yd. (3.66 m) of 45- to 54-in. (1.15 to 1.37 m) wide lining fabric
- 4 standard pillows
- 3 yd. (2.7 m) solid fabric for pillow backs and welts
- 12 yd. (11 m) of ¼-in. (6.4 mm) welting filler

You Will Also Need

Tape measure, yardstick, marking pencil, cutting shears, scissors, sewing machine with zipper foot, matching thread, sewing needle, iron and ironing board, access to professional quilter

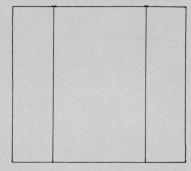

1. Cut and sew fabric for quilting. Measure length and width of top of bed. Measure thickness of mattress and add twice this measurement to bed length. Add three times mattress thickness measurement to width of bed (to accommodate back tuck-down, and front tuck-in) and add 10 in. (25.5 cm) for puffing caused by quilting. Place one width of fabric in center and add pieces at head and foot, matching printed design at seams and overall design to alcove lining (if applicable). Stitch seams. Check for matching. Press seams open. Send complete seamed amount of fabric out for quilting. (Extra fabric will be used for fronts of pillows but should be quilted in one piece.)

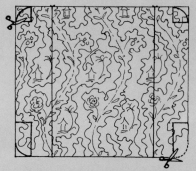

2. Cut quilted fabric. From fabric returned from quilter, cut exact rectangle based on measurements above (without allowance for quilting).

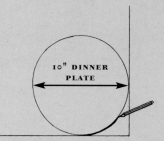

Round off corners. An easy way to do this is to use a dinner plate as a pattern. Cut away corners. Cut these shapes in unquilted bedspread fabric, adding seam allowance. Stitch in place, making sure direction of design is correct and front tuck-in is longer than back.

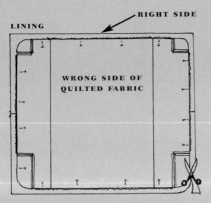

LINING

RIGHT SIDE

WRONG SIDE OF QUILTED FABRIC

3. Cut and sew lining.
Seam lining to make same-sized rectangle as bedspread. Leave 12-in. (30.5 cm) gap in one seam for turning. On large space, lay quilted bedspread on lining fabric, right sides facing. Pin together. Cut lining same shape as bedspread.

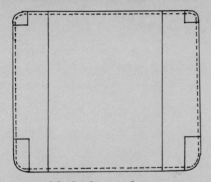

4. Assemble bedspread.
Sew around edge of bedspread. Turn right side out through gap. Hand sew gap. Lightly press edge. Topstitch all around bedspread 1 in. (2.5 cm) from edge.

5. Cut pillow fronts.
Measure pillow forms. Cut shapes in quilted fabric, centering design.

6. Cut pillow backs.
Cut same shapes in solid fabric.

7. Make welting.
Cut bias strips in solid fabric to make up enough yardage to go around all four pillows. Join into one strip and press seams open. Lay welting cord in strip and, with zipper foot, enclose cord in bias (see instructions for making welting in chapter 2).

8. Add welting.
Sew welting to fronts of pillows, finishing as instructed in chapter 2.

9. Assemble pillows.
Sew fronts to backs of pillows, leaving gaps for turning. Turn right side out. Stuff in pillow forms. Slip-stitch gaps by hand.

10. Finishing.
Place bedspread on bed matching one-way design to alcove (if applicable). Tuck down top, bottom, and back (side) against wall. Tuck front (side of bed) under mattress. Place pillows across back, or in pairs at top and bottom.

The coverlet and large pillows on this alcove bed in a summer cottage have been quilted by stitching around the printed design. The eaves and walls surrounding the bed are covered in the same linen fabric. Simple yellow cotton sateen curtains are slung on a rail above the bed.

Assembled from sample scraps of rayon satin from a drapery store, this bridal-looking patchwork quilt was made by Ella Kruger. The baby figure on it is an eighteenth-century Japanese decoy doll. Decoy dolls were often used to protect heirs when princely families traveled in brigand-infested areas.

Quilts, which are padded, come in many different designs and can be made with many different techniques, from white-on-white designs to trapunto. Patchwork quilts are the most familiar. Though patchwork is an age-old craft, it is still popular. Many designs have become classics over the years: "diamond in the square" is a bold, simple Amish design; "Joseph's coat" is a zigzag effect; "plain" has no decoration except two colored bands at the border. Many design names reflect the country life, in which making patchwork helped occupy long winter evenings: "sunshine and shadow," "checkerboard," "granny's garden," "broken dishes," "goose in the pond," "pinwheel," "windmill blade," "raising the log cabin," "chimney sweep." Though the sturdiest patchwork quilts were made from cotton, from 1860 to 1900 some more affluent households produced silk crazy quilts embellished with feather-stitched embroidery. Quilts were made of any fabric scraps available, from silk bands that came on cigars to feed sacks. Early American and especially Amish quilts are now regarded as important folk art.

Sheets, the mainstay of the linen closet, have been made of silk, linen, cotton, hemp, man-made fibers, and various blends of the above. Sheets can be perfectly plain or embellished with one or two simple rows of drawn-thread work at the hem. They can have embroidered edges or embroidered turned-down corners. The robber barons at the turn of the twentieth century had sheets embellished with their monograms or crests, such as Jacob Astor's rooster insignia, part of Françoise Nunnallé's collection of antique household linens, which can be seen at her Manhattan shop. We are all lured by the quality and stylishness of beautiful bed linens.

Fine drawn thread work and surface embroidery embellish this flounced voile pillowcase.

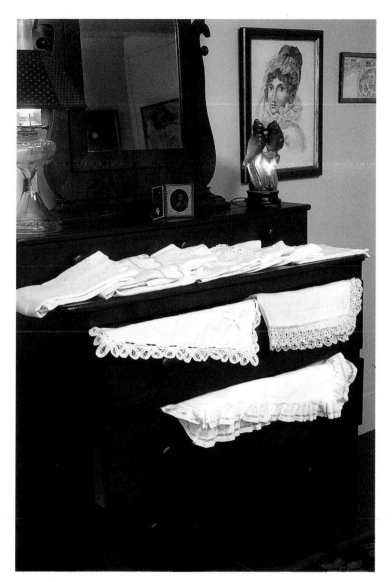

On this chest of drawers made in New Bedford — hence the whale-shaped supports for the looking glass — are a variety of pillowcases, some old, some contemporary.

Pillowcases are where bed linens can really go to town. Smaller and more visible than sheets, they can be covered in lace and embroidery. The well-dressed bed may have bolsters, square European-sized pillows, flounced king-sized pillows, and several small embroidered boudoir pillows, not counting a ribbon-bedecked neck roll—all at the same time.

Pillowcases are sometimes called pillow slips, as they are usually put on top of plain pillowcase linings. Proud German housewives had "parade pillowcases"—*Parade Kissenuberzug*—which were

This embroidered,
monogrammed, and
scalloped *Parade
Kissenuberzug,* or
"parade pillowcase," is
open at both ends. It
was part of a 1913
European trousseau.
Pillow slips of this
kind were used by
house-proud German
women to dress up
regular bed pillows
when not in use.

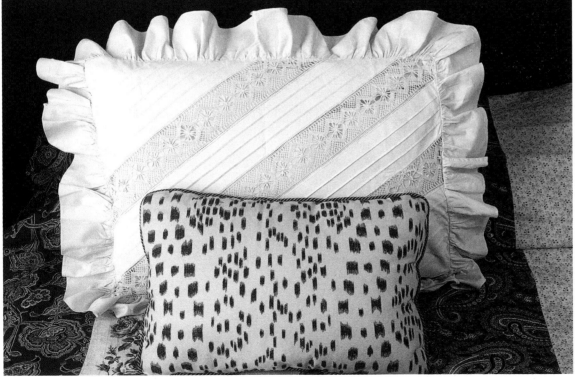

This vintage pillow-
case, part of the
early-twentieth-
century trousseau of a
Russian woman, Yeltea
Brodsky, is decorated
in diagonal tucks with
ecru lace inserts.

An antique crib quilt gets an airing draped on a garden statue.

open at both ends, often monogrammed, and slipped on for show only during the daytime, as in the photograph on page 86. Modern versions of this type of pillowcase can be found buttoned or tied on one or both ends.

There was a time when no self-respecting lady would have a bed that wasn't scattered with lace-covered boudoir pillows. Perhaps they are not quite as popular as they were in past decades, but these frothy confections can give a glamorous quality to a bed.

Some linen closets include baby layettes, christening robes, even vintage doll clothes, as well as wedding gowns packed away in tissue paper for daughters or granddaughters to cherish — and wear if they want to. When I was preparing for our oldest daughter to be born, I was told I needed a layette.

Having no idea what a layette was, I asked a friend in the garment district, where I was then working designing sportswear. "It is not," he said, "a brief encounter!"

The linen closet in a baby's nursery can include washable acrylic or cotton baby blankets, crib bumpers, woven or knitted sheets that fit the crib mattress, soft, small washcloths, and terry towels with hood corners. Françoise Nunnallé recalls rose-colored crepe de chine sheets richly appliquéd with ecru lace ordered by a grand household at the end of the last century for a mother's laying-in.

Curtains may also find a space in the linen closet, whether draperies that have been replaced (it is almost impossible to part with well-made draperies, even if the decor has completely changed) or simple door curtains, shower curtains, café curtains, short

Simple Lace Curtains

When measuring the width of a window for curtains, measure 1 inch (2.5 cm) beyond the outside edges of the window frame, as the double curtain rods—one for the curtains and the other for the valance—should extend beyond the frame.

The lace curtains in the photograph opposite were made from white lace fabric with a large flower design. Lace fabrics have a distinctive design, and this must be taken into consideration in planning the size of hems and valances for lace curtains. Care should be taken to match the underside of the hem to the outer fabric so that the lace design does not look muddled. Tiebacks can be made from a single strip of lace the width of the dominant motif and pleated at the ends into white plastic rings to be looped onto 1-inch (2.5 cm) angle hooks—found at upholstery suppliers. Elastic loops would work instead of rings, and a nail with a large head or a pothook would work equally well as an angle hook.

When using lace, it is a good idea not to make the curtains or valance too full, or the design of the lace will be lost. Each curtain for the window here was cut from one width of 45-inch (1.15 m) wide fabric for a window 30 in. (76.2 cm) wide by 33 in. (83.82 cm) long.

Materials
- 6 yd. (5.50 m) of 45-in. (1.15 m) wide lace fabric
- Double metal curtain rod expandable to 50 in. (1.27 m)
- Four 1-in. (2.5 cm) angle hooks
- Four ½-in. (12.7 mm) plastic or metal rings
- 2 lead upholstery weights covered in white fabric

You Will Also Need
Tape measure, yardstick, scissors, marking pencil, sewing machine, matching thread, sewing needle, iron and ironing board

1. Measure window.
Decide height of valance. Fix rod hardware to wall. Measure from this to floor for height of window. Measure 1 in. (2.5 cm) beyond window frame on either side for width of window.

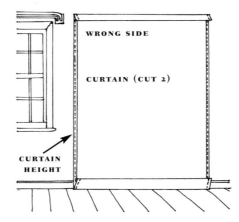

2. Cut curtains.
To window height measurement, add allowance for bottom hem so lace will match (5 in. [12.7 cm] for lace shown here) and 2 in. (5.1 cm) for top rod pocket (matching is less essential at the top, as it will be covered by valance). Cut two pieces this length by full width of fabric.

3. Sew curtains.
Press ½-in. (12.7 mm) side hems and topstitch. Press bottom hem and topstitch. Hand sew weights into leading edge hem. Press top pocket hem and topstitch.

4. Cut valance.
Cut strip of lace 60 in. (1.53 m) long and 15 in. (38 cm) wide, bearing in mind that undersides of hems should match outer sides. (A valance is generally an eighth of the length of the curtain.)

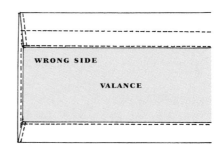

5. Sew valance.
Topstitch ½-in. (12.7 mm) side seams. Press at least 2 in. (5.1 cm) for bottom hem, matching show-through of lace design, and topstitch. Press 3 in. (7.6 cm) for top hem, matching lace design, and topstitch. Sew another row of stitches 1½ in. (4 cm) above this stitch for rod pocket. (Rod pockets on curtains and valance are intentionally wider than rods to avoid tearing lace.)

6. Cut tiebacks.
Cut two strips 5 in. (12.7 cm) wide (or suitable width for lace design) by 25 in. (63.5 cm).

7. Sew tiebacks.
Sew narrow hems all around both sides of both ties. Pleat or gather short ends of ties. Hand sew rings on at either end of tiebacks.

8. Assemble curtains.
Slot curtains onto shorter rod. Place rod on inner part of hardware. Slot valance onto longer rod, with 1 in. (2.5 cm) heading, and place on outer part of hardware. Hammer two angle hooks at baseboard. "Dress down" curtains. (This is an expression used by upholsterers to smooth curtains into graceful folds.) Sew a ring to outer edge of curtain to fit on baseboard angle hooks so curtain is under slight tension. Hammer other angle hooks into frame at sill height. Loop tiebacks onto angle hooks and arrange curtains gracefully.

Design Ideas
Curtains like this could also be made of voile, batiste, eyelet, dotted swiss with lace edging, or a combination of textured sheer fabrics appliquéd one on another.

In this tiny attic bedroom, a bedspread covers the top of the bed and has a gathered flounce that goes all the way to the floor. A matching pillow sham covers the bed pillow. Decorative pillows include one made from an old white-on-white quilt and another made from a crocheted mat. Simple lace curtains veil the window.

curtains to go under sinks, or frothy point d'esprit confections to embellish kidney-shaped dressing tables.

A very elegant bedroom closet may have a series of matching accessories such as those found at world-famous linen emporiums like D. Porthault: covered coat hangers of various weights and sizes, matching lavender sachets, covered shoe trees, and shoe holders.

Multiple shoe holders are a convenient way to store shoes in a closet. When making your own, pick a fabric that will look good in the bedroom, even though it will only show when the closet door is opened. Choose a binding fabric that enhances the base fabric or ties into the decoration of the room.

The shoe holder pictured on page 91 holds seven pairs of shoes, which was as many as would fit onto the door comfortably. Make the size of the shoe

Multiple Shoe Holder

Materials
• 4 yd. (3.65 m) of patterned fabric
• 3 yd. (2.74 m) of interfacing
• ½ yd. (46 cm) of solid fabric for binding, *or* 14 yd. (12.8 m) ready-made binding
• Thin wooden hanger

You Will Also Need
Tape measure, scissors, marking pencil, sewing machine, matching thread, iron and ironing board

1. Cut basic shape.
Cut two pieces in patterned fabric 17 by 57 in. (43.2 cm x 1.47 m). Cut one piece in interfacing. Lay front patterned piece on interfacing and sew raw edges together all around. Keep back separate to be joined in step 8.

2. Cut pockets.
For pockets, cut patterned pieces 9 by 29 in. (23 x 73.3 cm). This is width of base plus 1½ in. (4 cm) for pleats on either side of each pocket. Cut two pieces for each pocket needed. Cut one interfacing for each pocket. Lay interfacing between patterned pieces and edge-stitch all around raw edges. Notch center of each pocket piece at bottom.

3. Cut binding.
Cut a strip of solid fabric 3 by 27 in. (7.6 x 68.5 cm) for each pocket. These can be on straight grain rather than usual bias, as they will be sewn onto straight fabric. (Or use ready-made bias tape.) Cut binding piece 3 in (7.7 cm) by 3¼ yd. (3 m) on straight grain to outline holder, and another piece 3 by 20 in. (7.6 x 51 cm) on bias to go across curved top and bind hole for hanger hook. Press binding in half lengthwise to 1½-in. (4 cm) width.

4. Sew binding to pockets.
For each pocket, lay raw edges of binding alongside raw edges top of pocket piece and sew with ¼-in. (6.4 mm) seam. Trim seam. Turn binding to wrong side so that binding is slightly broader than on right. Press. Stitch from right side in groove between binding and patterned fabric, catching folded edge of binding on wrong side at same time.

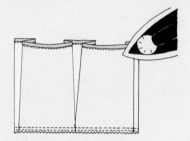

5. Make pocket pleats.
For each pocket, press 1¼-in. (4 cm) pleats at sides and either side of center notch. Sew pleats along raw edge at pocket bottom. Zigzag, pink, or overlock along bottom to finish seam, which will be inside pocket.

6. Attach pockets.
Sew each pocket at bottom to patterned front fabric, which is interfaced, by folding under finished seams, pinning each in place to get placement correct, then topstitching. Sew sides of pockets

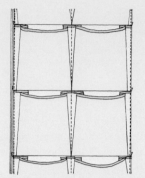

to patterned front fabric, raw edges to raw edges. Sew through vertical center of pockets, pinning first. (This is where check fabric is convenient, because match can be verified.)

7. Bind across bottom.
Using same method as in step 4, bind bottom of holder base front and interfacing together. Sew ½-in. (12.7 cm) separate hem on back of holder bottom so that hanger can later be inserted and removed.

8. Bind sides.
Sew edges of front to back, pinning first, then bind sides as in step 4.

9. Cut curved top.
Lay hanger along top of holder. Draw curve of hanger on fabric. Cut shape. Notch ½ in. (6.4 mm) on either side of center along top curve for hanger.

10. Bind top.
Sew binding across top, but stop at first notch, sewing binding only on front and interfacing to next notch, then finish binding all three fabrics to end of curve. Hand hem ½-in. (12.7 mm) space between notches at back for hanger hook to poke through.

11. Finishing.
Slot in wooden hanger.

Design Ideas
• Make shoe holder from scraps of
  fabric to give a patchwork effect.
• Pockets can be sewn on flat
  instead of having pleats at the
  sides. They can hold single shoes
  or even pairs if pockets are big
  enough.
• An alternate way to hang shoe
  holder is to keep the top of holder
  straight and slot in slim dowel rod
  between front and back to keep
  top straight. Sew simple fabric
  loops into both top corners. Affix
  screws or hooks into closet door
  to hang.

holder bear some relationship to the size of the door on which it will hang. If you prefer fewer pockets, adapt the measurements accordingly. The size of the pockets can be varied, smaller for children's shoes and larger for men's shoes.

If the fabric you select is patterned — or checkered like the one in the photograph — make the design of the repeating pockets match or relate to the base onto which they will be sewn. Using a plaid or check fabric is a mixed blessing: On the one hand, every square is marked, like graph paper, so cutting is easier. On the other hand, everything must match correctly; mistakes will show. With plain or allover patterned fabric, matching is not so crucial.

Binding can be made single or double, or it can be purchased ready-made in a limited range of colors. The binding serves as a border for the patterned fabric. If preferred, it can be eliminated, with the pockets and sides of the holder simply hemmed.

Handkerchiefs have figured in many stories from romances to murder mysteries, from *Othello* to *Rebecca*. Every female, from little girls to grandmothers, had a handkerchief case to hold her hand-hemmed or lace-edged handkerchiefs before the general onslaught of paper tissues. Men's handkerchiefs were equally important. Handkerchief linen was the finest to be found. Men's handkerchiefs can still be bought in a baker's dozen and look best with a discreet monogram. Silk kerchiefs tucked into the breast pocket are still worn to give color to a plain business suit.

*This cranberry-and-cream-colored multiple shoe holder
was made in checked linen to go with the bedroom.*

ABOVE: *A variety of handkerchiefs are stored in this nineteenth-century "gothick" wall cabinet.*

ABOVE, LEFT: *A handkerchief commemorating the accession of George VI is framed as a picture and used here as a tray for demitasse.*

LEFT: *The hangings and buckram-stiffened valance for this four-poster bed were made from an early-nineteenth-century cotton print. They were lined with printed sheets that match the bed linen, and the edges were bound with solid-colored polished cotton.*

OPPOSITE: *Next to this well-dressed bed, with its pink and cream embroidered linens from Anichini, is a skirted bedside table covered in gold-colored silk moiré. This bedroom was designed by Michael La Rocca for a Southampton show-house. (Photo by Dennis Krukowski.)*

Black, white, and red wallpaper with a border gives a sophisticated look to this country bathroom. The linen closet has a louvered door for ventilation.

This bathroom, decorated in a scheme that combines light gray and pale aqua, is shared by two young girls.

Commemorative handkerchiefs were once the souvenirs that dish towels have become. If souvenir handkerchiefs are of any serious age and visual interest, they can be framed as pictures. I have a blue-and-white one saved by my mother from the Boer War, and I use a commemorative handkerchief of the 1936 accession of George VI and Queen Elizabeth (now the Queen Mother) both as a picture and as a coffee tray.

A marble-topped washstand was a permanent fix-ture in the bedroom until this century. On it would be a basin and ewer, with lace-edged towels hung on rods at the sides. As indoor plumbing developed, a guest bedroom might be equipped with its own sink. Bathrooms have come a long way since those days. Now we have almost as many separate bathrooms as bedrooms. Bathrooms have become luxurious re-treats where one can conceivably spend a whole evening in self-indulgence—exercising, bathing, applying nourishing creams, and coloring hair.

Fingertip towels from an early-twentieth-century trousseau hang in a New York bathroom of the same period.

BELOW:

LEFT: *This hand towel of the pre–World War I period is richly embroidered with the figures of a woman and a bird.*

CENTER: *This 1913 pale green linen towel is embroidered with a bunch of grapes set on drawn-thread work surrounded by an elaborate frame border.*

RIGHT: *A linen hand towel worked with tape embroidery and pale green satin-stitched dots.*

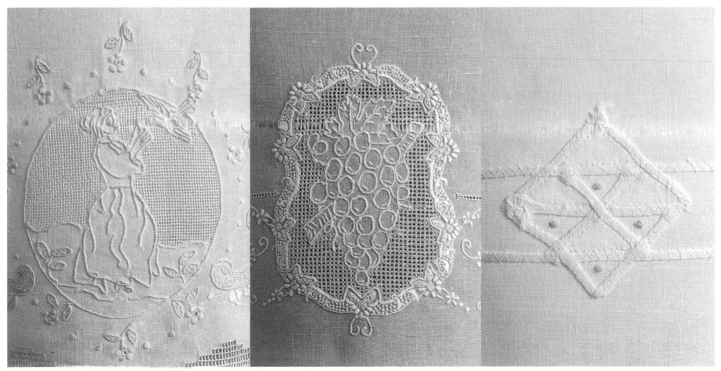

Under-Sink Curtain

The fabric yardages given here are for a 30-inch-long curtain and a 36-inch rod. As it's unlikely your measurements will be exactly the same, adapt these amounts as necessary.

The solid yellow binding in the photograph was chosen to pick up the distinctive color of the playbills used as wall decoration in this bathroom. The binding is double so that it can be applied totally by machine. If applied as single fabric, the binding would have to be hand hemmed on the wrong side. The binding is sewn to the leading edges that meet in the center and to the bottoms of the curtains.

Materials

- 2 yd. (1.8 m) of 50- to 54-in. (1.27 to 1.37 m) wide fabric
- ½ yd. (46 cm) of plain cotton for binding
- One 36-in. (91.4 cm) brass rod ⅜ in. (9.5 mm) in diameter
- Brass hardware holders

You Will Also Need

Yardstick or right-angled ruler, marking pencil, scissors, sewing machine, matching thread, iron and ironing board

1. Measure space.

Put hardware and rod in place under sink, leaving at least ¾-in. (19.1 mm) space above rod for curtain heading. Measure from top of rod to floor to calculate height of curtains. The one pictured was 30 in. (76.3 cm). Add 3 in. (7.6 cm) for bottom seam allowance, top heading, and rod pocket. Measure length of rod to calculate fullness of curtains—a width for each curtain is a general rule.

2. Cut fabric.

On large flat space lay fabric face down. Decide placement of fabric design. Mark two widths at height established in step 1 and cut. Curtains pictured are 33 in. (84 cm) high by 52 in. (1.32 m) wide.

3. Cut binding.

Lay solid fabric face down. On true bias (45-degree angle), cut strips 3½ in. (9 cm) wide for binding to make up 7¾ yd. (7 m). Join strips. Press seams open. Press bias in half lengthwise to form doubled strip 1¾ in. (4.5 cm) wide.

4. Apply binding.

Lay binding on leading edge of curtain, raw edges matching. Sew, taking ½-in. (12.7 mm) seams, without stretching binding. At bottom corner, pleat binding to form miter and continue across

bottom of curtain. Trim seams to ⅜ in. (9.5 mm). Turn binding over to wrong side so ½ in. (12.7 mm) shows on right side. Binding should be slightly wider on wrong side. Press. From right side, stitch in the groove between binding and curtain, catching folded edge of binding on wrong side. Repeat for second curtain. Make sure binding is on mirror-image edge.

5. Hem sides.

Press in ½ in. (12.7 mm) twice on sides and stitch.

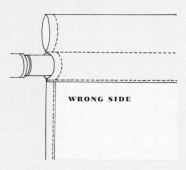

6. Hem top.

Press ½-in. (12.7 mm) hem to wrong side along top of curtain. Fold over 2 in. (3.1 cm) and press. Machine stitch edge of hem. Stitch another line ¾ in. (19.1 mm) above first stitch line for rod pocket. Repeat with second curtain.

7. Finishing.

Press both curtains. Slot rod in pockets. There should be ½-in. (12.7 mm) headings above pockets.

Design Idea

Another way to attach a curtain to the bottom of a sink is to glue one side of Velcro to the bottom of the sink, sew the matching Velcro to the fabric, and attach.

A curtain can be easily made to hide cleaning supplies and toilet paper under a sink, as in this powder room, papered with playbills.

The bathroom closet holds linens of all sizes, from gigantic terry bath sheets to piqué fingertip towels. Towels, like other household linens, can easily be made distinctive by adding homemade touches. Designers know the trick of sewing washable colored cotton ribbons or braids to towels to blend them with the color scheme. Colorful knotted or bullion fringes can be sewn to the hems of towels and facecloths. Lace can be added to one or both ends of hand towels and monograms added by hand or by machine.

The bathroom itself can be made more glamorous by hiding the plumbing fixtures and cleaning supplies under the sink with an under-sink curtain. Held in place with ever-useful Velcro or slotted onto a rod, a curtain can be readily laundered and changed with the decor.

The under-sink curtain in the photograph above was made in two parts for easy access and hangs from a polished brass rod set under the sink. The antique marble sink above it was found at a country sale. It is bordered with small decorative tiles.

Every family member has his or her own bathrobe or dressing gown, but when guests come to stay, it is a welcoming idea to provide them with a robe. Traveling in France, I noticed that many hotels had towel-like bathrobes, made simply, that were perfect to put on after a bath. Instructions for making simple robes, cut in straight pieces, are provided on the next page. You may find it practical to cut two at the same time.

Brightly colored towels are stacked on bathroom shelves in a summer cottage.

Simple Bathrobe

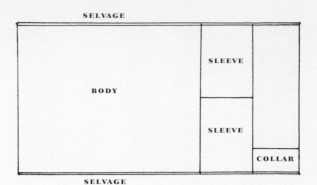

To make this simple one-size bathrobe, all you need is terry cloth, bought by the yard, and some heavy ropelike cord for ties. Using a zigzag or overlock attachment is the most efficient method for finishing the seams inside, however, when I made my first robe like this, I sewed French seams, and they worked perfectly well even in the thick terry cloth.

Materials
- 2¼ yd. (2 m) of 46-in. (1.17 m) wide terry cloth
- 1½ yd. (1.4 m) of ⅝-in. (15.9 mm) diameter cotton rope

You Will Also Need
Yardstick, marking pencil, cutting shears, scissors, sewing machine, matching thread

1. Cut robe pieces.
Lay terry cloth on large flat space. Measure and cut piece 52 in. (1.32 m) long for body. Bottom and top of robe are on selvages. Measure and cut two pieces 23 by 18 in. (58.5 x 46 cm) for sleeves. Cuff edges of sleeves are on selvages. Measure and cut one piece 18 by 12 in. (46 x 30.6 cm) for collar. One edge of collar is on selvage.

2. Hem fronts.
Sew ½-in. (12.7 mm) hems on raw edges of body of robe to clean-finish fronts. Notch center back.

3. Slash to set in sleeves.
Starting from selvage, cut slash 8 in. (20.5 cm) deep 12½ in. (32 cm) in from stitched hems on both sides for sewing in sleeves.

4. Set in sleeves.
Lay raw edge of sleeve on raw edge of slash, right sides facing. Sew seam to end of slash. Keep needle down, turn fabric, and sew up other side of slash. Underarm of sleeve will be on fold. Repeat with other sleeve. Zigzag or overlock seams.

5. Sew shoulders.
Sleeve seam and shoulder are sewn in one line. Lay raw edges of sleeve together, right sides facing. Sew seam all the way to neck. Repeat with other sleeve. Zigzag or overlock seams.

6. Cut rope.
Divide rope into two even pieces. Tie knots 3 in. (7.6 cm) from one end of each piece and fluff ends to make tassel effect. Bind other end of each piece with thread to prevent raveling.

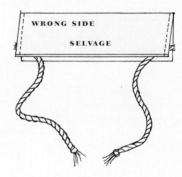

7. Make collar.
Fold collar in half lengthwise, right sides facing. Lay bound ends of rope against raw edges of ends of collar, ½ in. (12.7 mm) up from edge. Stitch across ends, catching rope. Notch center back of collar on raw edge side (not selvage side).

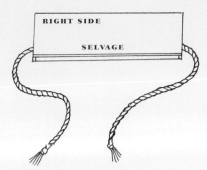

Turn collar right side out.

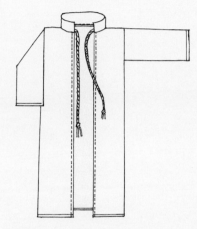

8. Set on collar.
Pin center back of collar to center back of robe, right sides facing. Pin front of robe to front of collar. Pin to distribute small gathers between. Sew raw edge side of collar to robe. Pin selvage edge of collar over seam to hide it. Topstitch along collar, trapping raw edges inside collar.

Design Ideas
Though these robes are traditionally white, it is a nice idea to use colored terry that goes well with a guest room. This way, when a robe is laundered, it will always find its way back to the right room. If you can't find terry to coordinate, bind the fronts with colored cotton.

Draped on this princely falconer statue is a simple bathrobe inspired by similar ones found in French hotels.

OUTSIDE

Patios, Pool Houses, and Gardens

THOUGH WE DON'T THINK OF the great outdoors when we think of household linens, there are many linens that we use for outside life: beach towels, pillows, picnic tablecloths and napkins, gardening aprons, and kneeling pads. Many of these outdoor items can be easily made. If you cannot find ready-made pool or beach towels to your liking, it is a simple matter to buy terry cloth by the yard—it comes plain and printed—and add a simple colored cotton binding.

Plain extra-large bath towels can be embellished for use as beach towels with a strip of fancy cotton braid or a luxurious cotton bullion fringe. Nowadays, bath towels come in many wonderful, bright colors that look spectacular in bright sunlight. Washable ribbon can be used as binding and even applied to form initials. When my daughter Emma was young, a friend embroidered her name in bold, contrasting chain stitch on a large square towel made from colored terry cloth piece goods. The hem around the edge was embroidered with a herringbone stitch. It was a favorite towel and is still in use.

Pillow covers and seat pads that last outdoors (at least for some time; no fabric is impervious forever) can be made from striped awning canvas, which has a water-resistant finish. To help cushions stand up to the weather even longer, have the canvas treated

Towels for swimming are stacked on shelves under a staircase in a summer place.

with spray-on water repellent, which forms a plastic coating on the cloth.

Some people prefer to use all white for outdoor pillows to avoid fading. Make them unique by embellishing the plain white or natural canvas with a three-dimensional effect such as seams, tucks, piping, or trapunto. Piping can be added in a color that will enhance the decoration in a pool house or gazebo. To make outdoor pillow covers easy to remove, use Velcro. If you use zippers, be sure to use heavy plastic ones to prevent rusting.

During the hot, lazy days of summertime, every country porch needs a rocking chair or swing seat. Because many rocking chairs are made of wicker, which is hard and uneven, a pad is a nice way to soften the seat. Over the years, the pad shown in the photograph on page 107 has been covered in many different fabrics, because eventually they all fade or get worn out. Here the pad is shown covered in the same awning stripe as the pillows on page 105.

Awning stripe is ideal for a seat cover because, though too narrow for many projects, it is the right width for a pad like this, and the fabric has a special

A simple set of white-painted wooden shelves displaying large decorative shells holds batik sarongs and swimming trunks, ready for a summer vacation.

Beach towels and swimming gear are piled on a metal-backed porch seat decorated with fern motifs.

sun- and water-resistant finish, which stiffens the fabric but also makes it long lasting.

The mitering on the throw pillows has not been used on this seat pad cover. The stripes have been kept simple because the thick pad is shaped to fit the curve of the chair. As it is not an even square, mitering the stripes would be complicated—though not impossible—so it has been avoided.

Gardening is a spectacularly growing trend in America. Garden clubs are popping up all over the place. Gardening and plant shops are proliferating. New gardening magazines and catalogs arrive every week. We are all becoming more sophisticated about planning, landscaping, and organizing our gardens. Avid gardeners can use aprons, pinafores, elasticized anklets and pull-on sleeves to protect from the ever-present danger of insect bites, and scarves for the head.

Keep all fabric scraps that have pretty floral or leaf motifs. They can be cut into squares or circles with pinked edges and, tied with a ribbon, used to dress up plastic plant pots for presents or local tag sales and charities.

Anyone who gardens knows that some form of pad, whether individual knee pads, a kneeler, or an easy-to-cart-around kneeling pad, is essential if you are really going to get down to earth. Traveling around country houses and gardens open to the public in England, my husband and I bought a handsome kneeling pad at a National Trust gift shop. It was made of burlap stenciled with the National Trust acorn print. Until recently, the pad has held up to an awful lot of hard wear, but finally I decided to give it a new lease on life by covering the heavy three-quarter-inch rubber interior with new fabric.

I could have bought burlap and stenciled it using a homemade lino or potato print, then covered it with transparent vinyl to make it possible to sponge off. Instead, I found a perfect green-toned acorn print on a sturdy furnishing-weight cotton. A Velcro opening makes it easy to remove for laundering. As a companion piece, I made a matching gardening apron using a one-size-fits-all design with plenty of pockets to hold trowels, twine, and packets of seeds. This is a useful, simple-to-make combination that is a wonderful present for fellow gardeners.

Mitered Striped Pillow Covers

The amounts given here will make two pillows, because what you cut from one style of mitering, you can use for mitering on the other style of pillow. Because awning stripes are often printed, not woven, and have their surface finished only on one side, it is far more economical to use a balanced stripe rather than an uneven, one-way stripe. Awning stripes, however, are made in narrow widths, suitable for deck chairs. If the pillows will be used outside and get damp, polyester filling is advised.

The front of each pillow cover is made by joining four pieces, with the stripes matching so they form designs. The stripes must match or the effect is lost. Take plenty of time to cut accurately, marking true right angles. There are many ways to combine stripes, so use your imagination.

A chunky welt frames the square pillow cover. Depending on the fabric used, it may be possible to find the right color of ready-made welting by the yard. If not, make welting from plain fabric cut into bias strips and filled with welting cord (as described in chapter 2).

The back of each pillow should be made in plain, unmitered stripes. This makes it possible to disguise the Velcro opening along a stripe.

Materials
- 2½ yd. (2.3 m) of 30-in. (76.4 cm) wide awning stripe
- Two 18-in. (46 cm) square pillows to cover
- 4 yd. (3.66 m) of ready-made welting *or* ½ yd. (46 cm) of plain fabric for welting
- 1 yd. (91.4 cm) of ¾-in. (19.1 mm) matching Velcro (½ yd. per pillow)
- 4 yd. (3.66 m) of ¼-in. (6.4 mm) welting cord filler, if needed

You Will Also Need
Brown paper for pattern, right-angled ruler, marking pencil, cutting shears or scissors, sewing machine, matching thread, iron and ironing board

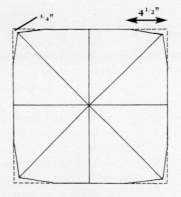

1. Make template.
In brown paper, cut 18-in. (46 cm) square. Shape off corners ¾ in. (19.1 mm) as shown, then draw lines dividing square into four diagonally, vertically, and horizontally. Cut a triangle out using diagonal lines.

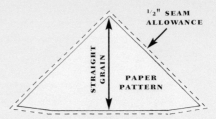

Using this triangle as a guide, cut another triangle, adding ½-in. (12.7 mm) seam allowance to each side, but redraw vertical line from apex of triangle to center of base.

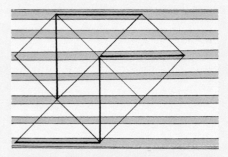

2. Cut front mitered pieces.
Lay fabric on flat space (right side down only if stripe design shows on wrong side). Decide on center of stripe design. Lay triangle-shaped pattern on fabric so vertical line tallies with chosen center line on fabric. Mark around pattern. Repeat as shown until four identical pieces are marked. Interlocked with them will be four more identical triangles with the stripe going across rather than down. Check that all triangles are perfect and that the two sets of triangles are identical as you cut them out. Stack both sets separately.

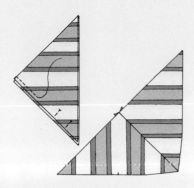

3. Stitch front pieces.

To stitch miters, pin two matching triangles together, right sides facing on bias, matching stripes exactly. Sew together, taking ½-in. (12.7 mm) seam. Check for match. Press seam open. Repeat with other pair of triangles.

Outdoor pillows can be made from awning-striped canvas, which stands up to sun and weather. Interesting designs can be formed by mitering the stripes.

Lay both joined sets together, matching at center and pinning carefully so all stripes match. Stitch and press seam open.

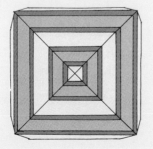

Repeat with second set of triangles.

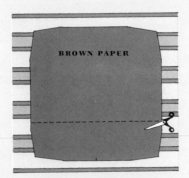

4. Cut backs.

In brown paper, cut 18-in. (46 cm) square. Shape off corners. Decide best place on stripe design for opening, whether at center stripe or nearer to edge of pillow. If fabric has a 2-in. (5 cm) wide solid stripe, as the one in the photograph does, this is an ideal place for Velcro opening. Cut brown paper square across at decided opening.

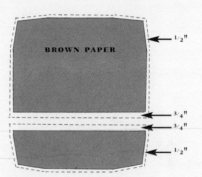

Using these shapes as guides, cut two new pieces of brown paper, adding ¾ in. (19.1 mm) to both sides of Velcro-opening cut, and adding ½ in. (12.7 mm) all around rest of both pieces. Cut in fabric.

(continued on following page)

5. Add Velcro.
Sew Velcro to underside of larger piece for opening on back cover, folding raw edge under Velcro, and to top side of smaller piece, covering raw edges as Velcro is added.

6. Add welting.
Place welting at center of one side of front of pillow, raw edges together. Using zipper foot, sew welting all around edge of front of pillow cover, taking ½-in. (12.7 mm) seams. Finish welt seam as described in chapter 2.

7. Assemble pillow cover.
Sew front to back with right sides facing, using previous stitching as guide.

8. Finishing.
Turn pillow cover right side out using Velcro opening. Stuff in pillow form. Close Velcro.

Seat Pad for a Porch Rocking Chair

The seat pad shown has a 4-inch (10.2 cm) thick pad. Adapt the measurements for the side gusset if your pad has a different thickness.

If a chair does not have a seat pad, you can make one from several layers of batting cut to the desired thickness and shape. Cover the batting with muslin cut to the dimensions of the seat pad cover.

Materials
- 2 yd. (1.8 m) of awning stripe cotton
- Seat pad to cover
- 20 in. (51 cm) of ¾-in. (19.1 mm) wide Velcro
- 3 yd. (2.74 cm) ready-made welting or ½ yd. (46 cm) of plain fabric for welting
- 3 yd. (2.74 cm) of ¼-in. (6.4 cm) welting cord, if needed

You Will Also Need
Brown paper for pattern, marking pencil, ruler, scissors, sewing machine, matching thread, iron and ironing board

1. Make pattern.
Cut piece of brown paper slightly bigger than inside of chair seat. Lay in seat, pushing paper down to form creases around back, sides, and front of chair where arms are. Cut paper pattern. Fold through center to make sure both sides match and cut notch at center front and center back. Recheck pattern in chair.

2. Cut top and bottom of pad cover.
On flat space, lay fabric wrong side up (as long as stripe design is still discernable). Decide where center of design looks best. Lay pattern on center line of stripe. Add ½ in. (12.7 mm) all around before cutting. Cut two identical pieces.

3. Cut side gusset.
Decide which part of stripe will look best for gusset. Measure 10 in. (25.5 cm) on either side from

center back notch and make two more notches. This is for back gusset piece, which will be cut in two pieces with Velcro opening. Measure from one of these notches all around front and back to other notch. Add 1 in. (2.5 cm) to measurement.

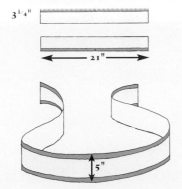

Cut one piece this length by 5 in. (12.7 cm) wide in selected gusset stripe. Cut two pieces 21 in. (53.5 cm) long by 3¼ in. (8.4 cm) wide for back gusset. These should match front gusset when Velcro has been sewn in place. Notch middle of front gusset and middle of back gusset.

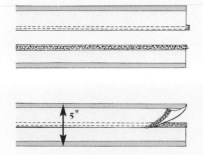

4. Sew in Velcro.
Sew Velcro to underside of one side of gusset opening, folding raw edge under Velcro, and to top side of smaller piece, covering raw edges of gusset as Velcro is stitched.

Every rocking chair can be made more comfortable with the addition of a seat pad. This one is made from striped awning fabric to match the mitered pillows in the previous photograph.

5. Add welting.
Make welting as described in chapter 2. Starting at center back, sew welt all around top and bottom of seat pad cover, finishing off as in chapter 2.

6. Sew in gusset.
Sew front part of gusset to back part, taking ½-in. (12.7 mm) seams.

Pin and sew gusset to top and bottom of seat pad cover, matching front notch of gusset to center top of pad cover and matching back notch of gusset to center bottom of pad cover. If needed, make small pleat where Velcro is inserted.

7. Finishing.
Turn seat pad cover right side out using Velcro opening. Stuff in seat pad form.

The apron is constructed in a simple way and will fit any size and shape of person. The neck loop is all in one with the ties and can be adjusted to accommodate any size chest and waist. The pocket placed at the hem is divided into sections and deep enough to hold tools but not so deep that you lose the seed packets or twist 'ems for tying plants in the bottom.

I happen to like the idea of a pretty floral chintz kneeling pad, but to keep it clean, it is a good idea to cover it with a clear vinyl plastic — the sort that is used for shower curtains — which is hard wearing and can be sponged clean.

I was once commissioned to line several woven-wood pie hampers with a classic checkered furnishing linen (held in place with Velcro, which made it removable for washing), containing matching tablecloths and napkins, for Jacqueline Onassis to give as gifts to her friends. The hampers were so attractive that I made one for our family. It has been a mainstay ever since for summer picnics in the meadow of our New England country house and for alfresco suppers at our local open-air theater.

For this project, I used good quality linen like the classic check on page 113, which is often used by upholsterers for the back of bergères — deep armchairs with closed arms and seat cushions — and other solid-backed chairs. A natural-and-white combination would look very good too. A regular cotton gingham check would also do, providing it is firm enough to sit well on roughly cut grass. A patterned cloth is much easier to keep looking clean than a solid color.

An unusual gardening pad can be made using a bold floral chintz covered with transparent vinyl.

Gardening Apron

The fabric shown has an oak leaf pattern, but choose any fabric you prefer, so long as it is hard wearing, fairly heavy, and washable. If the design on the fabric is obvious, try to match the tool pocket to give a professional, finished look to the apron. The tie can be made in three pieces for economy in cutting, as the joins will be hidden in the curved armhole casings, which are cut as facings. The tie is long enough to tie in a bow at the back, or to cross at the back and tie in a knot in front.

Materials
• 1 yd. (91.4 cm) of 45- to 54-in. (1.15 to 1.37 m) fabric

You Will Also Need
Marking pencil, scissors, ruler, sewing machine, matching thread, iron and ironing board, large safety pin for threading tie

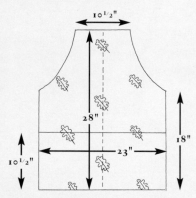

1. Cut apron.
Mark apron shape on wrong side of fabric following measurements in illustration. Cut pocket 10½ in.

(27 cm) deep — it will be 9 in. (23 cm) deep finished — matching pocket piece to apron. Cut three pieces for tie 1 yd. (91 cm) by 3 in. (7.6 cm). Cut facings using apron armhole shape as pattern, making them 2¼ in. (6 cm) wide.

2. Make tie.
Join three tie pieces together to form one 8¾ foot (2.7 m) long piece. Press in ½ in. (12.7 mm) all around, then fold tie in half length-wise and topstitch around edge.

3. Sew pocket hem.
Press ¼ in. (6.4 mm) then ½ in. (12.7 mm) across top of pocket. Topstitch hem.

4. Attach pocket.
Sew pocket to bottom hem, matching right side of pocket to wrong side of apron, allowing ½-in. (12.7 cm) seam allowance. Add another stitch, then pink to finish seam that will be inside, or zigzag if machine has capability. Turn pocket to right side and press to knife edge, that is, so seam is on exact edge.

5. Sew apron edges.
Sew raw side seams of pocket to raw side seams of apron at edges. This holding stitch will be hidden in hem. Press in first ¼ in. (6.4 mm) then ½ in. (12.7 mm) for hems on both sides and across neck, and topstitch.

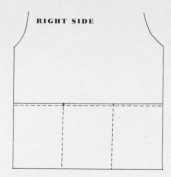

6. Topstitch pocket.
Divide pocket into three sections and mark vertical lines with pins. Topstitch through-and-through. Backstitch by machine at top of pocket for reinforcement.

7. Add facings.
Press ½ in. (12.7 mm) to wrong side of each facing piece on longest curve and topstitch to wrong side to finish raw edge. Press to wrong side ¾ in. (19.1 mm) at top and bottom facings and topstitch. Trim away protruding points. With right sides facing, stitch facings to armholes, taking ¼-in. (6.4 mm) seams.

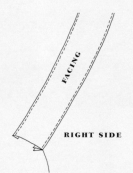

Turn to right side and edge-stitch facing through-and-through to both seam allowances to ensure facing lies smoothly to wrong side and cannot show out. Press facing to wrong side.

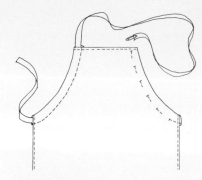

Mark line 1⅛ in. (3 cm) in from finished edge of armhole with pins and topstitch through-and-through armhole, catching facing so as to form casing for tie. Machine back-stitch at start and finish of stitching for reinforcement.

8. Finishing.
Thread tie into casing formed by facings using large safety pin. Press apron.

This early-twentieth-century Maine garden chair—originally designed as a trellis—holds a gardening apron and matching kneeling pad made in an oak leaf–printed linen. Photographed at folk art collector Raymond Saroff's farmhouse.

Kneeling Pad

If your fabric has a lot of white background, line the print with a plain white or natural fabric so that the rubber mat underneath does not show through. If you only have enough of a remnant for the front of the pad, make a plain back, but use clear vinyl on both sides. (The instructions below assume that the back of the pad is plain.) The welting and hanger can be in a complementary color, preferably darker than the print if you wish to "fence in" the printed design.

Materials
- ¼ yd. (23 cm) of fabric, chintz or something more sensible
- ¼ yd. (23 cm) plain white or cream fabric to line chintz, if necessary
- ¼ yd. plain cotton for welting and back of pad
- 1¼ yd. (1.14 m) thick welting cord
- 1¼ yd. (1.14 m) clear heavyweight vinyl plastic
- ½-in. (12.7 mm) thick rubber pad

You Will Also Need
Marking pencil, scissors, sewing machine, matching thread

1. Cut pad.
If rubber pad is not already cut to shape, cut it into a long oval or lozenge shape, and then use as pattern.

2. Cut fabrics.
Allowing for ¾-in. (19.1 mm) seams, cut floral and plain white fabric (if needed for lining), backing, and two pieces of vinyl. Cut bias strips 1½ in. (1.4 cm) wide to make into welting. Cut piece of welting fabric 3 by 10 in. (7.6 x 25.4 cm) for hanger.

3. Sew vinyl to cover.
Using regular foot, sew vinyl on top of right side of chintz and (if needed) plain white under it, stitching at the edge of the raw edges. Make sure there are no threads or foreign bodies between chintz and vinyl. Sew vinyl to back of pad cover.

4. Sew hanger.
To make hanger, fold in ½-in. (12.7 mm) seams and press. Fold in two lengthwise, forming clean-edged strip 1 by 10 in. (2.5 x 25.4 cm). Topstitch along long sides of hanger. Pin in place on right (chintz) side of pad cover.

5. Make welting.
Change to zipper foot and make welting (see welting instructions, chapter 2).

6. Assemble pad cover.
Attach welting to top (chintz) side of pad cover, trapping hanger in place. Sew top of pad cover to bottom, leaving 8-in. (20 cm) gap for turning.

7. Finishing.
Turn cover and insert pad, making fabric lie smooth under vinyl. Slip-stitch gap by hand.

Lined Picnic Hamper with Cloth and Napkins

Amounts are for one tablecloth, four generous napkins, and lining for a traditional woven-wood pie hamper.

Materials
- 3½ yd. (3.20 m) of 45- to 54-in. (1.15 to 1.37 m) wide check linen
- Pie hamper
- 2 yd. (1.8 m) of ¾-in. (19.1 mm) Velcro

You Will Also Need
Tape measure, marking pencil, scissors, sewing machine, glue, matching thread, iron and ironing board

1. Cut and sew picnic cloth.
Cut square in linen using width of fabric as measurement. Press in narrow hems and stitch.

2. Cut and sew napkins.
Cut four pieces 22½ in. (57 cm) square if using 45-in. (1.15 m) fabric; 18 in. (46 cm) if 54-in. (1.37 m) wide fabric. Press in narrow hems and stitch.

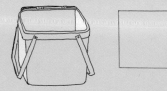

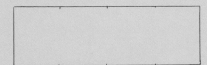

3. Cut lining.
Measure around inside top of hamper and from top down to base. Make long rectangle pattern from brown paper for lining sides using these measurements. Measure length and width of inside bottom of basket and make pattern for lining base. From remainder of linen, cut side and base pieces of lining, adding ½-in. (12.7 mm) seam allowances.

4. Sew lining.
Sew long lining piece together, matching checks if possible at side seam. Sew base piece. Press seams open. Around top, sew Velcro to wrong side, hiding raw edge.

5. Attach Velcro to hamper.
Glue other side of Velcro to inside of hamper around top edge.

6. Finishing.
Attach lining Velcro to hamper Velcro. Press and fold picnic cloth and napkins and place in hamper.

A picnic hamper is made by lining a wooden pie hamper with fabric, including a matching picnic cloth and napkins.

Care, REPAIR, and STORAGE of LINENS

OUSES of size and importance have always had linen rooms for ironing and repairs. Sometimes these rooms have floor-to-ceiling cupboards with deep shelves and drawers. Usually there are irons, ironing boards, and sewing tools. Maintaining linens was — and is — important, requiring patience and skill.

The fact that pieces of actual woven linen have survived from the days of ancient Egypt is almost miraculous. There's no great trick in preserving a granite statue, but fabric is so much more ephemeral! Silk is even more perishable than linen or cotton, as it rots easily. Wool has to be protected from moths; all fabric has to be kept from animals like mice and even squirrels, who love to use it for their nests.

In the distant past, laundry was done in rivers and streams. Dirt was beaten and pounded out of fabric rather than washed out with soap. Linens were laid out to dry on the grass or on hedges so the bleaching action of the sun combined with the chlorophyll of the greensward would produce sweet-smelling fabric. Later, soap was invented by combining lye leached from wood ashes with fat. Many country people still make their own household soap, which is efficient because it hardens as it ages, making it last a long time.

For centuries, household washing was traditionally done on Mondays, and often took most of the day. I remember as a child the rather comforting, steamy smell of laundry being boiled in a huge gas-heated copper tub, which was kept under a lift-up wooden draining board in the scullery. Diamond-shaped soap flakes were scattered in the tub, and the linens were swished around and pounded with a bleached wooden plunger. I don't remember bleach ever being used; it tends to damage fabric anyway. The wash would be taken out, rinsed in a galvanized metal tub, and run through the "mangle" — our name for the wringer. Buttons on shirts, which were mother-of-pearl in those days, were turned in so they wouldn't be broken; children's underwear had rubber buttons, and there were linen or thread buttons on pillowcases. All buttons from worn-out shirts and dresses were kept in a button bag. It was a great treat to play with the button bag; it contained buttons that had been on my great-grandmother's wedding dress.

We were at the mercy of the weather for drying. Washing lines crisscrossed our small back garden, and sagging sheets were lifted by wooden props, tall poles with V-shaped notches — I wish I could find them now! At the first sign of rain — which was frequent — everything was brought indoors and hung on racks that were raised by a pulley system to the high kitchen ceiling. A fire was almost continually going in the kitchen; it warmed an oven, heated water upstairs, and kept a kettle simmering on a swivel trivet for tea. When the sheets were still slightly damp, they were ironed on an old blanket and sheet

PREVIOUS PAGES:
A linen room is an important element in a well-run large house. This room is in Rosemont, an 1804 plantation house in Virginia belonging to the Byrd family. A no-nonsense space with a bare lightbulb and curtainless window through which the light can stream onto plants put here for the winter, the room is used for sewing, ironing, and storing sheets, lace curtains, quilts, coverlets, fragile lace-trimmed nightgowns and peignoirs, and the other linens that a large and bustling house collects. (Photo by Dennis Krukowski.)

The linen room at Elmwood on Quaker Hill, Pawling, New York.

laid on the kitchen table, then stored in piles up- stairs in the "airing cupboard," where the copper hot-water heater kept them dry. After World War II, most of our family linen was washed by a profes- sional laundry. It would be picked up and delivered once a week in a big oblong box made of thick, dark blue cardboard, fastened with a leather strap. In- side, the white linens were wrapped in pink tissue paper, tied with string. My father's surplice would always be on top, as it creased most easily, being

made of fine linen. There was a clean one every week, ready for the Sunday service. Each item had our family initials embroidered in the corner in red thread. I still have some of them, even precious lace pieces one would never dream of sending to an or- dinary laundry nowadays.

In the 1950s, launderettes and detergents (causing many environmental and septic problems) were the thing. I was living in the big city. It felt ever so mod- ern going — on the back of a Lambretta — to watch

Sheets laid out on the grass to dry and bleach naturally in the sun.

the laundry spinning in washing machines that were doing all the work. By the more environmentally aware 1970s, detergents became less harmful. There is even a new device on the market now—a not-inexpensive plastic ball that works through a form of electromagnetic force, making the wash possible with no soap or detergent. Back to our beginnings!

Now most households and apartment buildings have their own washing machines and dryers, and it seems as if every piece of linen, often regardless of its care label, goes in.

Drying linens outside is still the best method. Whether sheets are laid out on the grass or hung on a washing line over grass, the benefits far outweigh the use of chemical bleach, which wears out fabric, and dryers, which make cloth dingy and stale smelling. Only forty years ago, rural housewives would lay their linens out in full moonlight so that they would be bleached, but not as harshly as by sunlight.

Today not everyone has access to an outdoor drying space. We tend to settle for the convenience of dryers, especially in bad weather. There is also an assumption that hanging clothes on a line is somehow demeaning. My husband, Keith, says that hanging washing on the line—right outside our formal drawing room—is one of his greatest pleasures: "One of the best parts of the weekend."

As with all household chores, there is a skill to hanging linens on a line. Overlap two items using one clothespin to save time; stretch items taut on the line so they don't droop—the wind will blow them dry more quickly, and they will be less wrinkled; stretch each seam and hem as you pin them. I'll never forget seeing a well-reviewed Broadway play in which a hardworking rural mother hangs washing on a line. Obviously, the actress and director had never seen real laundry hung, she did it so carelessly.

In the 1960s, all but the finest bed linens were made of drip-dry and no-iron blends. Pure cotton, linen, and silk became luxuries as the mass market succumbed to the convenience of polyester. By the end of the decade, a casually tousled, handmade look was in style, which was reflected in the household linens of the time. The iron more or less ceased to be used. Pure cotton—which always existed in the more expensive linen emporiums—made a comeback in department stores in the 1980s and 1990s. Many people wash and tumble-dry cotton sheets and put them straight on the bed without ironing. They like the soft feel and ignore the wrinkles.

I prefer smooth sheets, along with cloth napkins and pressed jeans, so I've learned to love ironing. To me, ironing is a pleasure, as it is a pleasure for Keith to hang the clothes out to dry on a sunny day. There is something quietly pleasing about doing your own ironing. Fresh-smelling real linen sheets and pillow-cases have to be dampened to an exact degree prior to ironing. The best way is to puncture holes in the metal lid of a juice bottle and use it as a sprinkler. Fold the dampened linen tightly in a plastic bag for a couple of hours. Ironing goes even more easily if the sprinkled linen is kept in the freezer until you are ready to iron.

Sheets should be ironed first on the wrong side of the top hem, especially if the hem is at all fancy, then folded in half, quarters (and eighths if large) lengthwise, then folded in half, quarters, and eighths to form a neat rectangle. This way they are easier to place evenly on the bed, by matching the fold to the center. I have never found a really fool-proof way of ironing and folding fitted sheets; they never sit quite as neatly on the shelf. All linens should be used in rotation to ensure regular use. Their positions should be changed from time to time so that the folded edges of sheets do not dis-color due to oxidation.

Table linens require starch—not every time they are washed, but fairly frequently. Spray starch will do in a pinch—though the aerosol canister is not to be encouraged, and I know several people who get a bad allergic reaction to spray starches. Regular liq-uid starch is more economical and can be made light, medium, or very stiff, according to your need. Vintage damask tablecloths look best when stiff with starch, the way they would have been origi-nally. I like to see table linens with creased-in folds, but others prefer their tablecloths to be absolutely creaseless.

When ironing, inevitably there is an occasional scorch mark. If the fabric is not damaged, there are several ways to try and remove scorches:

- Sponge scorch mark with cotton soaked in per-oxide.
- Lightly brush scorch mark.
- Do not wet, but place item in sunshine.
- Make paste of baking soda and water, apply to scorch mark, and place item in sun.
- Rub scorch mark with lemon juice and place item in sun.
- Mrs. Beeton (whom I trust) gives the most ex-otic recipe: "Boil ½ a pint of vinegar, 2 ozs of fuller's earth, 1 oz of dried fowl's dung, ½ oz of soap and the juice of 2 large onions together to the consistency of paste; spread the composition thickly over the dam-aged part, and if the thread be not actually con-sumed, after it has been allowed to dry on, and the place has subsequently been washed once or twice, every trace of scorching will disappear." I have two vintage hand towels badly scorched from a heating unit and all the ingredients but the fuller's earth (currently on back order from my local drugstore); I hope this concoction will do the trick.

To remove a soiled spot without leaving a ring, rub in cleaning fluid and sprinkle it with baby pow-der or cornstarch while it is still wet. When it is dry, gently brush off the powder. To remove rust stains, use RIT rust remover. (RIT has several products that work well, such as dye remover and fabric whitener, and they are available in most supermarkets.)

If there is grime on a really old, precious fabric, do as many museum conservationists do: dab it with distilled water on a pad of clean fabric, gently push-ing the dirt out from the between the fibers. This takes time and patience, but it will not harm the fabric.

Wool blankets are usually dry-cleaned. Hang them on the line outside to get rid of the cleaner's

Airing blankets on a line out of doors gets rid of the closed-in smell when they have been boxed or held in cedar closets or mothballs for the summer.

OPPOSITE: In rural areas, kitchen towels used to be put on hedges to dry.

A good way to dry a heavy crocheted or knitted coverlet is to lay it out in an exact square on a perfectly flat space in the open air.

chemical smell, or the cedar closet or mothball smell if they have been stored during the summer. Too much dry cleaning is ruinous to many fabrics. Some wool blankets can, with skill, be washed satisfactorily in cold water.

Duvets can be washed, and are best tumble-dried to fluff the down. Cotton crocheted, knitted, or lace coverlets and curtains can be washed, but they are best not put in the dryer. If there is any cut or loose thread, they will unravel. Instead, lay them out to dry on a flat surface.

Many households used to have stretchers for drying the lace curtains that were fashionable in the past. The curtains were fixed onto pins on the stretchers so they would dry to the right size and shape. Depending on the type of lace, curtains can stretch considerably if hung when wet. We had some tea-dyed lace curtains that gained more than twelve inches in length and lost six inches in width when I made the mistake of hanging them to dry. Usually, they can be blocked back into shape on a flat surface.

The best way to dry delicate cotton or linen embroidery is to lay it when still damp on a flat surface, smooth out every wrinkle with your fingertips, spread the lace edging into shape or comb out the fringe, and let it dry. If you iron complicated embroidery, such as cutwork or elaborate drawn-thread work, you run the risk of breaking threads with the tip of the iron. The same smoothing-out system applies to fancy handkerchiefs. This method does not work with anything that has frills and flounces. On these, use an iron to thrust as far as possible into the gathers.

As well as an iron, every linen closet should have sewing equipment for mending. It is here that the saying "A stitch in time saves nine" really applies. If you machine stitch over the hem of a towel when the stitches first start to crack, it will last twice as long. The same applies to the edges of coverlets, blankets, and sheets, which wear out the most quickly of all.

Sheets wear out first in the center. Large households and some hotels make their sheets last as long as possible by splitting them down the center when worn. The selvages are then joined into a narrow center seam, and the raw edges at the sides are hemmed.

In our household, everything gets recycled. Worn pillowcases become cleaning rags and dusters.

This circular cloth, heavily embroidered with cutwork and surface stitches, has been stretched out on a smooth surface with fingertips while still damp so that it will dry without wrinkles.

OPPOSITE: *Linens can be dried out of doors well into the winter. Sometimes they freeze into stiff boards, but they can be folded and ironed quite easily. Here is a fancy lace tablecloth drying in the snow after a festive party.*

Sewing Sheets Sides to Middle

Materials
• A freshly laundered sheet, slightly worn in the center

You Will Also Need
Cutting shears, sewing machine, matching thread, iron and ironing board

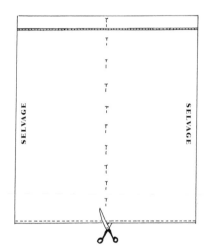

1. Cut sheet.
On a large flat space, fold sheet in half lengthwise. Cut along fold.

2. Seam sheet.
Place the outside selvages together, right sides facing. Sew ¼-in. (6.4 mm) seam. Press seam open.

3. Make hems.
Press in ¼ in. (6.4 mm) twice on raw edges at sides for hems. Stitch hems. Press sheet.

Sewing Tips
• Every sheet wears in a slightly different way. If the most worn part is not on the exact center, adapt these instructions to your particular sheet.
• Individual rips can often be caught together and mended by machine. Sew like a French seam so no raw edges show.
• Holes can be patched using fabric from worn-out sheets.

Threads are picked from the hems of blankets and rewoven to darn holes invisibly. Old needlepoint is repaired and worn embroidery reworked. The good parts of an old patchwork coverlet may become pillow covers. Even fluff from the dryer is used as batting in old quilts. Mending is a healing, sentimental gesture that gives a hands-on sense of the past.

Patchwork quilts, especially antique quilts, are generally hard wearing, but they do require some care. Do not hang patchwork quilts permanently in bright light. Light will destroy them. Keep them in quilt chests or drawers except when in use. If they are used on beds, turn them at least once a month. Keep the blinds closed when the room is not in use. Do *not* dry-clean antique quilts at local cleaners. If they are precious, go to a specialist cleaner. If you launder a quilt in a machine, use the gentle cycle, with no harsh soap. I have seen precious old quilts ruined by professional cleaners and launderers. Sooner or later fabric wears out and stitches pull out if quilts are much used. Fortunately, there are several ways to repair the damage:

• Patchwork quilts can be repaired again and again, almost until a new quilt is made! Just add new patches as they wear out. You can't easily make new patches fold under each other as in the original, but as patchwork quilts are wrinkled by the quilting, small discrepancies do not show badly.

• Professional menders often sew net under worn fabric to reinforce it.

• Save fabric scraps for patches. Keep them in a rag bag, such as a small laundry bag.

• Use fabrics as close to the original as possible — thin cottons rather than thick textures and old, soft fabric to mend old quilts. Do not use man-made blends unless it is a modern quilt.

Patchwork quilts come in many varieties. This is a type often called a "yo-yo quilt." New pieces of fabric can be added if the original fabric wears away.

• Press the pieces first, as they will be crumpled in the rag bag.

• Use the back of prints if necessary to get a faded effect.

• Sew with a short fine needle.

• Restitch the through-and-through quilting stitch after applying a new patch.

• To repad tiny spaces where the batting has gone or clogged to the side, use fluff from the dryer and push it into place with a needle or pin.

GLOSSARY

Allover: A printed fabric covered with a small repetitive design.

Antimacassar: An old-fashioned term for a piece of cloth—plain or decorated—placed over the back of a chair to protect upholstery (originally made to protect it from a commonly used Indonesian-made hair-dressing oil called Macassar).

Appliqué: *See* Embroidery.

Awning stripe: A heavy woven cotton canvas, duck, or drill used for awnings, beach umbrellas, or cushions, with stripes either woven into the fabric or printed or painted on the surface. Sometimes called a *Roman stripe*.

Balanced stripe: A stripe arrangement that follows the same design to both right and left—having a center with the stripes on either side mirroring each other—as opposed to a one-way stripe, where the design only runs in one direction.

Baldachin: A draped, crown-shaped structure over a bed.

Basket weave: Two or more warps and wefts used as one in a plain weave to give the effect of a woven basket. Often used for curtaining, as it is a loose construction. Hopsack, monk's cloth, and oxford are all made with basket weave.

Basic weaves: There are three basic weaves (as opposed to complex weaves)—tabby, satin, and twill, with many variations on these.

Batik: A printed fabric, originally from Indonesia, made by coating areas not to be dyed with wax, which is then removed. This technique gives a distinctive freehand design effect. Now the effect is often commercially duplicated.

Batiste: A fine, sheer mercerized muslin made of cotton or cotton blend and less often of spun rayon, sheer silk, or fine wool. Named after French linen weaver Jean Baptiste.

Bias: A fabric's true bias is at a forty-five-degree angle from the selvage.

Bias binding or bias tape: Fabric cut into narrow strips on the bias with the raw edges folded in, used for trimming and binding. Bias binding can be bought prepackaged in a variety of colors and in several widths. It can also be made at home.

Braid: Decorative trimming that can be topstitched or hand sewn to decorate, outline, hide a seam, or trim a shelf, or used as a tie. Braids come up to four inches wide and in many weaves and colors.

Buckram: A scrim fabric with a stiff finish used as interlining and in millinery.

Café curtains: Unlined curtains covering the bottom part of a window for moderate privacy. Used primarily in kitchens.

Calico: An inexpensive cotton fabric that originated in Calcutta, India, with a resist-printed (also called discharge-printed) background, covered in simple small-scale designs in two or three colors. Designs can be tiny, simple flowers or geometrics and have a distinctively naive American-country look.

Cambric: Soft, closely woven white cotton with a gloss on one side from calendering. Originally made in Cambrai, France, and used for church embroidery and table linen. Useful for aprons and handkerchiefs. (*See also* Chambray.)

Canvas: A heavy, strong cotton or

linen; also an open-mesh fabric that comes in various qualities used for needlepoint embroidery; also an unbleached linen canvas used as interfacing.

Cashmere: A fine, soft, wool-like fabric made from the cashmere goat. The best quality is found in Tibet, the Kashmir province of India, Iran, Iraq, and southwest China.

Centering: Establishing the focal part of a printed pattern on a fabric before cutting an item from the fabric.

Chambray: A cotton shirting with a colored warp and white filling, named after the French town of Cambrai, where it was originally made. (*See* Cambric.)

Chenille: A fabric made from chenille yarn, which is fuzzy (*chenille* is the French word for caterpillar). Useful for bedspreads, throws, cushions, and robes.

Chevron: A twill weave going in different directions to create a herringbone effect.

Chintz: Printed cotton fabric used almost exclusively in interior decoration; it often has a glazed finish.

Chou: A crumpled puff of fabric used to accent curtain swags, or the top and/or bottom of chandelier-chain covers, or overhead bed drapery. (From the French for cabbage.)

Compound weaves: Fabrics with more than one warp and more than one filling.

Cording: Twisted or braided cord in a number of sizes and variations, either applied to or inserted into upholstery, cushioning edges and adding color and definition. When cording is over an inch in diameter it is often called rope.

Corduroy: Any one of many variations of velvety-pile fabrics woven into vertical ribs, or wales, and then cut. Uncut corduroy has a ribless pile.

Cotton: There are many types of cotton grown, depending on soil and climate, which affect the color, strength, length, and other characteristics of this vegetable fiber. *Sea island* is the finest, long-stapled, white, and silky, now raised in Central America and Mexico. *Egyptian, American pima cotton* (a cross between the previous two), *supima, American peeler, American* (the world's largest crop), *Peruvian, Indian, China,* and *acala* are other types.

Count: Refers to the number of ends and picks (the threads in warp and weft) per inch in a woven cloth. A square cloth is one that has an even number of threads in warp and weft.

Crash: A course, irregular fabric made of linen, cotton, or blends, woven from thick, uneven yarns. Often used for draperies and table linens.

Crepe de chine: A sheer, flat crepe of silk or man-made fibers.

Cross-grain: *See* Grain.

Damask: A fabric created by combining twill and satin weaves. Damask is reversible, limited to two colors—warp and waft threads—and used for formal table linen.

Denim: A rugged fabric with a twill weave, usually in a shade of blue. The name comes from de Nîmes—"of Nîmes"—the French town where the cloth was first made. Good for bedspreads and pillows in children's rooms or for use in sporty, country, or ranch-style rooms.

Dimity: A heavy everyday cloth in the eighteenth century and a medium-weight fabric in the nineteenth, this is now a lightweight, unpretentious fabric, usually with vertical ribs. It has many household uses, including slipcovers and cushions.

Dobby: A weave with small, symmetrical, repeating motifs.

Dotted swiss: Also known as *point d'esprit*, a sheer cotton embellished with small dot motifs.

Drying cloths: Towels for drying china, cutlery, and other utensils, also known as tea towels, kitchen towels, dish towels, or glass cloths. (Kitchen towels are generally on a roller system and used for drying hands.)

Dupioni: Strong slubbed silk formed from double cocoons called dupions.

Dust ruffles: Gathered, pleated, or straight lengths of fabric that hang from the mattress to the floor on a well-dressed bed.

Duvet: French name for a down-filled comforter that hangs over the sides of the bed rather than

A linen tray cloth shows a handmade lace edging and inset combined with cutwork.

A small simple natural-linen mat with embroidered corners is part of a set that came in several sizes for plates and glasses.

A closeup of drawnwork, or hemstitching, can be seen on this heavily starched hand-pulled fringed tablecloth.

sitting on top, like an eider-down. A duvet usually takes the place of sheets and separate blankets.

Embossing: A design pressed into fabric with heat, rather like making a waffle.

Embroidery: Embellishing fabric with applied white or colored thread. Originally done by hand, nowadays much embroi-dery is duplicated on a schiffli or other type of machine. The many types include:

• *Appliqué:* Embroidery done when one fabric is cut into a shape and applied—often with fancy stitches—to another fabric to form a design. Some commercial appliqués with adhesive backing can be set in place with a hot iron.

• *Beadwork:* Designs formed by the application of tiny colored glass beads to a mesh canvas.

Done extensively in the nine-teenth century, beadwork was often combined with needle-point and used on pillows, footstools, pincushions, and bellpulls.

• *Colbert:* Embroidery worked on a net or mesh ground with fine thread.

• *Crewel:* Inspired by late-seventeenth-century English designs, this embroidery usually depicts leaves, vines, flowers, and animals by using wool on unbleached linen or cotton. Used extensively on bed hangings.

• *Cutwork:* Usually worked in white on white on cotton or linen. Shapes are cut out, then finished around the raw edges with a closely worked button-hole stitch.

• *Drawnwork:* Also called *drawn-thread work, hemstitching,* or *fagoting.* Threads are pulled out

of fine linen, then held together by thread in clumps to form simple ladderlike effects or twisted into more elaborate designs that can be horizontal and vertical, with various knot-tings of threads in between.

• *Eyelet embroidery:* Called *broderie Anglaise* in England and France, eyelet was origi-nally made by punching holes with a stiletto in fine white cotton and stitching around the holes to form repeating designs. Now eyelet is made by machine. It is characterized by small round or oval holes, often connected by surface embellish-ments. It is most typically white on white. Useful for small café curtains, boudoir pillows, dust ruffles, and bed hangings. (*See also* Eyelet.)

• *Needlepoint:* Worked with yarn —usually wool—on a mesh canvas using a blunted needle, stitches include bargello and cross-stitch — called gros point or petit point, according to size.

• *Smocking:* Lightweight fabric is gathered in even rows, then decorative surface stitches are worked to hold and stabilize the gathers. Most popular on little girls' dresses, but also used on curtains, bed draperies, lamp shades, and small items.

• *Stump work:* A padded, dimensional embroidery done since Elizabethan times. In the nineteenth century, a variation of the technique was called *Berlin work,* as it was a popular craft among German ladies. It is similar in some ways to quilting, but quilting uses an even layer of padding, while stump work is unevenly padded, with fabric puffed up to form images and then embellished. Antique stump work is rare and costly. Used for small decorative items, such as pictures.

• *Trapunto:* A linear quilting formed by trapping soft cord between parallel lines of stitching.

Eyelet: A small perforation in fabric often worked around with a buttonhole stitch or secured with a metal grommet, to hold a tape, string, or hook. (*See also* under Embroidery.)

Felt: A wool or wool-blend fabric formed by matting fibers under heat, moisture, and pressure. A woven felted cloth is called *melton.*

Fiberfill: Polyester stuffing that can be bought in various forms — sheets to use in quilts and seat pads, small pieces to stuff into pillows, or pillow forms.

Filling: *See* Weft.

Findings: Buttons, linings, needles, ribbons, snaps, threads, Velcro, and other items needed to complete a sewing project.

Finish: The final treatment to give a fabric a desired effect, such as calendered, crease-resistant, embossed, glazed, lustrous, napped, mercerized, Sanforized, waterproofed, etc.

Flannel: A cotton fabric, sometimes printed or woven in a fancy pattern, slightly napped on both sides to give a wool-like hand. Unbleached flannels are used as interlining and table felt.

Flax: *See* Linen.

Flounce: An embroidered border design.

Flour sacking: Plain-weave pure cotton, used in the past to make flour sacks and frequently reused by rural seamstresses, after having been bleached to remove as much of the printed-on labels as possible, for clothing and household linens. According to old timers, flour sacking was also made in gingham checks and calico prints.

Foam rubber: A material that comes in many weights and thick-nesses, used for seat padding, mattresses, kneeling pads, and more.

French corners: Also known as butterfly, gathered, or *Turkish*

Fashion designer Leamond Dean wore this underwear as a one-year-old in South Carolina. It was made by his mother from flour sacks and is stitched entirely by hand, including the buttonholes.

corners, these are the gathers or pleats at the corners of cushions that give a soft, rounded effect.

French seam: A seam sewn first on the right side, then sewn on the wrong side, trapping raw edges in second seam.

Fringe: Decorative trimming made of cut, looped, or knotted threads that hang from a heading. Varieties include:

• *Ball fringe:* Also called *bobble fringe,* it is made by clustering fringe yarns, then steaming them to form balls that can range from half an inch to an inch in diameter. Usually made of cotton, ball fringe can be home-dyed to use on towels, curtains, the edges of shelves, etc. Ball fringe is not generally used on luxurious pieces.

• *Beaded fringe*: Used mostly on curtains, beaded fringes come in colorless, crystal-looking beads; colored, translucent beads; wooden beads; and jetlike beads.

• *Block fringe*: Fringe made in recurring blocks of color.

• *Bullion fringe*: Heavy fringe made from twisted yarns that double back on themselves, forming a ropelike effect. Used mostly on the bottom of uphol-stered furniture, but the smallest variety can be used on towels.

• *Fan-edge fringe*: Also called *giselle*, fan edging is a supple, silky block fringe but has a soft zigzag edge formed with loops.

• *Knotted fringe*: Long fringe — from 3 to 12 inches — in which yarns are clumped together and knotted in various decorative ways. The best are hand knotted, but there are many machine-made versions. Can be found on good Turkish bath towels.

• *Moss fringe*: Sometimes called *brush fringe*, moss fringe is a full, thick, silky, straight-cut fringe, usually no bigger than an inch wide and usually inserted. It looks most effective when the fringe is doubled and therefore fuller.

• *Self fringe*: If the fabric you are using is suitable, you can pull threads out to make your own fringe.

• *Tassel fringe*: Fringe formed from small tassels.

Gathering: Also called *shirring*. This is a term for fabric that is stitched to ruffle and give full-ness. *Ruching* usually means gathering more than one line to give a puffed effect.

Gimp: A flat, narrow, woven trim-ming that comes in a variety of raised patterns; often used on wood-frame furniture to cover upholstery tacks, but also used in many decorative ways on walls, shelves, lamp shades, and pillows.

Gingham: Fabric woven to have a block or checkered effect. Gingham is usually made of cotton or cotton and synthetic, but can be silk. Readily avail-able in fabric stores, gingham comes in many colors and many check sizes. Items made of gingham tend to have a casual, country look.

Glass toweling: A plain-weave cotton or linen in which stripes or blocks of usually blue or red yarns give a simple design. Launders and lasts very well.

Glaze: A glossy fabric surface produced by heat, heavy pres-sure, chemical action, or a glazing substance. (Chintz is glazed.)

Grain: The direction of vertical threads or warp of a fabric. *Cross-grain* is the direction of the weft or horizontal threads.

Grosgrain: A ribbed fabric; also a ribbed ribbon that comes in many sizes and colors and is especially useful in home sewing.

Ground: The background of a fabric pattern.

Hand woven or hand loomed: Woven by hand rather than by a power-driven machine loom, giving an individual effect.

Hem: The finish on the edge of a cloth article. It can be accom-plished in many different ways: bound, hand sewn, hemstitched, machine stitched, rolled, etc.

Hemp: A cultivated herb of the mulberry family used to make fabric and cordage.

Herringbone: A weave in which twills, or diagonal weaves, alter-nate directions, forming a zigzag pattern. (*See also* Chevron.)

Holland: Also known as *shade cloth*. A plain woven linen or cotton that is often heavily sized and given an oil treatment to render it opaque. Used mostly for curtains and shades.

Huckaback (or huck): A heavy linen or cotton cloth with a honey-comb or waffle weave, used as toweling.

Interlining: A fabric inserted between the front and the lining of curtains, coverlets, or table skirts to provide body, warmth, insulation, and/or to prevent light from coming through.

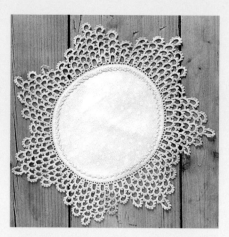

The lacy-looking edge of this doily was tatted by my great-aunts in the late nineteenth century.

The edge of this damask-centered doily is worked in hand crochet.

Intricate lace doilies were once a standard item in every kitchen linen drawer.

Jacquard fabrics: Named after Frenchman Joseph Marie Jacquard, these are large woven patterns made by programming looms using punched cards. Damask, for instance, is made on Jacquard looms.

Knife-edge: A term used to describe seat pads, pillows, and other fabric-made objects with no insert or gusset to add thickness at the edge of the shape.

Lace: Openwork fabric or edging often made from thread, cut and embroidered, or of woven tape, to give an open effect. Laces were originally hand-made and acquired their names from the areas where they were first made. Now many laces are imitated by machine. Varieties with distinctive characteristics include:
• *Point lace:* Made from thread by needle. Includes *Alençon* lace, *guipure*, and *venise* lace.
• *Pillow lace:* Made on a pillow using bobbins. Includes *Chantilly, Cluny, Nottingham,* and *Val* (Valenciennes).
• *Crocheted lace:* Includes hand-crochet and *Irish* lace.
• *Lace made with woven ribbons:* Includes *Renaissance* lace.
• *Lace appliquéd to net:* Includes *Brussels* and *Normandy* lace.
• *Schiffli embroidery:* Originated in Switzerland (*schiffli* means "boat" and refers to the shape of the shuttle on a schiffli machine). The lacy effect is produced by embroidering motifs on a net ground.
• *Lace darned in squares onto a mesh ground:* Includes *filet* lace.
• *Tatting:* Fine spider's-web effects made from thread worked by hand using a special double-pointed bobbin.

Lawn: A light, thin, usually white cloth made of combed cotton, originating in Laon, France. Sometimes woven with satin stripes, printed, or crinkled to form a plissé. Lawn is crisper than voile but not as crisp as organdy.

Leading edge: The edge of a curtain that faces another curtain and is often trimmed along that edge in some way.

Linen: Fabric produced from the flax plant, which has long fibers. Linen has natural luster and stiffness, absorbs moisture, does not soil quickly, and takes color well. Used extensively for household linens.

Lock stitch: A stitch that is often used to outline fabric designs when quilting. Unlike chain stitch, lock stitch will not pull out in one thread if it catches.

Marseilles work: White coverlets of sturdy cotton in intricate sculptural weaves, used as traditional bed covers.

Melton: *See* Felt.

Mm: Refers to the weight of Chinese silk. Higher numbers are heavier weights. Designers pronounce it "mumme" or "momme."

Moiré: Fabric with a watered-silk appearance. Originally produced by applying pressure from heated cylinders. Now available in woven or printed versions.

Mull: A fine, sheer fabric, usually cotton but sometimes silk.

Muslin: A term coming from Mosul, in Iraq, muslin has many meanings now (*see* Toile), but it generally refers to a simple, inexpensive woven cotton cloth. When unfinished, muslin is used for draping patterns. Finished, it is used for apparel and household linen. Muslin is usually natural color but can be dyed.

Nap: The direction in which the pile of a fabric is brushed, especially on velvets.

Needle board: A device used for pressing velvet without bruising the pile. Fine metal spikes are set into a flat, flexible pad, which is placed on a regular ironing board.

Nylon: A manufactured chemical fiber with many forms, uses, and trade names.

One-way: A printed fabric pattern that has one direction that is definitely "up."

Organdy: Very light, thin, transparent, stiff cotton cloth used

This dark-hued piece of patchwork uses the puff technique. Probably early twentieth century. (From the collection of Raymond Saroff.)

for bedspreads, pillow frills, and curtains (as well as party dresses). Crushes easily but can be ironed back to crispness. *Organza* is a similar fabric made of silk.

Ottoman: A silky fabric with ribs of unequal widths that run from selvage to selvage.

Paisley: A fabric design based on an Indian cone motif, named after Paisley, in Scotland, where soft wool shawls using variations of these patterns were produced to copy the more expensive originals made in India.

Palampore: An Indian word meaning "coverlet"; also a hanging typically patterned with a large tree-of-life motif.

Passementerie: Any type of cord, braid, fringe, or tassel used for embellishment.

Patchwork: Any number of techniques of joining small pieces of fabric together to produce a larger piece of cloth. Sometimes the pieces are sewn randomly, and sometimes they form intricate designs with specific names. Patchwork is often quilted, and patchwork names are associated with quilts. These include "basket" or "flower pot," crazy quilts, which are featherstitched random patches, "friendship," often with appliqués of hands, "log cabin," "mariner's compass," "pinwheel," "rocky road," "sawtooth," "schoolhouse," and "star of Bethlehem." Six- or eight-sided patchwork is a variation in which fabric is basted onto cardboard forms, then over-stitched together on the wrong side with tiny stitches, after which the cardboard is removed. *Yo-yo* patchwork is made when small circles of fabric are gathered around the edges, pulled tight, and hand stitched together at top, bottom, and sides so that the patchwork forms spaces between them. When the circles are puffed out with padding, it is called *puff* patchwork.

Pelmet: A decorative band, drape, or ruffle used to hide the pulley system on curtains. Also called a *valance*.

Percale: A high-grade sheeting with a fine, smooth, and lustrous texture used for bed linen. Can be given a no-iron finish.

Piece-dyed: Fabric that is dyed after having been woven. A "piece" refers to a fifty-yard length of fabric.

Pile: *See* Nap.

Pilling: The forming of tiny gatherings of fluff—"pills"—on the surface of a fabric made by the rubbing of fibers in wear.

Pillowcase linen: High-count, plain-weave, bleached linen with a smooth finish that washes well and has a cool feel.

Piping: *See* Welt.

Piqué: There are many varieties of piqué, from light to heavy-weight, but the best-known weave has a corded effect that runs down the warp of the fabric. Piqué is usually made of pure white cotton. The cords, or wales, can vary from pinwale to wales a quarter of an inch in width. Other weaves are bird's-eye, honeycomb (waffle), and variations on diamond-shaped weaves. Piqué is a crisp material to use in bathrooms and bedrooms.

Plain weave: *See* Tabby.

Pleats: Fabric that is folded and stitched—and often pressed—in a regular progression to control fullness. Types of pleats include:
• *Accordion pleats:* A simple up-and-down pressed fold like the pleats in an accordion box.
• *Box pleats:* Pleats that alternately change direction, forming boxlike pleats on the right side and inverted pleats or separated inverted pleats on the wrong side.
• *Crystal pleats:* Tiny, even accordion pleats.
• *Inverted pleats:* Two or more pleats that change direction, meeting to form a V at the top, where they are secured. A series of inverted pleats may form box pleats or spread-out box pleats on the reverse.
• *Knife-edge pleats:* A series of one-way pleats, usually pressed.
• *Pinch pleats:* Pleats bunched up into groups, or a series of single bunched-up pleats. These are usually found at the top of curtains, designed to control the fullness of the fabric, and can be made by applying commercially made curtain tape and hooks, or hand sewn.
• *Sun-ray pleats:* Accordion pleats that start small and grow wider, regardless of the grain of the fabric.
• *Unpressed pleats:* Any box, inverted, or knife-edge pleats secured at the top but left unpressed to form soft folds.

Plissé: A puckered finish on cotton, nylon, or rayon obtained by a caustic soda solution. The effect may or may not be removed after washing, depending on the quality of fabric.

Polar fleece: A fabric often made of recycled plastic with a fleece-like pile. It is supple, warm, and washable.

Polyester: A man-made fiber with various properties that can be combined with natural fibers to produce fabrics that are long lasting and easy to launder.

Poplin: A crisp, fine-weave cotton shirting that comes in a variety of colors.

Pongee: A type of unbleached, plain-weave silk similar to shantung.

Portière: A curtain hanging from a rod on a door or across a doorway to cut drafts.

Puddle: Fabric flowing onto the floor from a curtain or table skirt. The amount can vary from one to eight inches.

Quilting: Quilting is done by stitching two fabrics together with a batting between for warmth and to add dimension to the design. In the past, quilts were often made from previously stitched and embellished patchwork, and the top, batting, and lining were assembled at a quilting bee using a special frame. Nowadays, quilting can be sent out to be done professionally by machine, in allover patterns or to outline printed designs.

Railroading: A way of cutting fabric down the grain as opposed to the more orthodox method of cutting across the grain, which then requires matching the print on each seam. Railroading can save needless seams if the fabric design is nondirectional.

Ramie: A strong, inexpensive, lustrous Asian fiber.

Rayon: A manufactured fiber made of regenerated cellulose. Once considered downmarket because it shrank when washed, with improved manufacture, rayon is a soft, silky, much-desired fabric.

Rep: A weave similar to poplin but with a distinctive cross-rib cord. Used for dressing gowns.

Repeat: The length of a printed or woven fabric pattern before it repeats itself. Fabric with a large repeat is always more expensive to use because more cloth is required to match the print.

Repellent treatments: Treatments applied to fabrics to make them repel moths, mildew, or water. Very few are permanent.

Resist print (or dye): A method of creating a pattern on fabric by covering certain areas before dyeing, often with wax, which is then removed after dyeing. A series of dye baths can be used to create multicolored designs. (*See also* Batik, Wax print.)

A *selection of ribbons in a basket; also included are a double-fringed braid and a border of embroidered silk.*

Ribbon: Ribbons come in many shapes, colors, sizes, weaves, and fibers. Ribbon sizes are referred to by numbers ranging from #1, which is a quarter of an inch wide, to #40, which is three inches wide. Specialty ribbons can be even wider. Types of ribbon include grosgrain; Jacquard; picot-edged, which has tiny loops spaced along each selvage and gives a nice, old-fashioned effect; satin weave, some of which are single-faced, with the satin effect on only one side, but the best of which are double-faced, with satin weave on both sides; taffeta weave; velvet; and combinations of these varieties.

Rickrack: A thin, flat zigzag braid trim.

Right-angled ruler: A metal ruler 16 inches (approximately 40 cm) long in one direction with, at right angles to it, a ruler 24 inches (approximately 60 cm) long.

Roman stripe: *See* Awning stripe.

Rosette: A decorative circular confection made of fabric or ribbon used to punctuate draperies.

Ruche: Fabric that has been gathered on two edges, such as a ruched piping or a ruched area on a pillow, to give a puffed effect.

Sateen: A mercerized cotton fabric in a satin weave.

Satin: A weave with the warp being of the most precious thread, such as silk, and covering the weft in order to produce a lustrous surface with a dull back. There are many types of satin, with upholstery satin being the most useful in upholstery and curtains, satin crepe for bedspreads, and wash satin for sheets and pillowcases.

Seam: The joining together of two pieces of fabric by sewing. Common types include French seams, run-and-fell seams, and shirt seams.

Seersucker: A lightweight cotton, nylon, silk, or blend fabric woven on two warps—one slack and one tight—to produce the characteristic wrinkled appearance. Used often for bedspreads and blanket covers, as it needs no ironing. Seersucker is permanently wrinkled, but plissé, which is heat or chemically set, is not.

Self fabric: Matching fabric, such as for a welt, cut from the same cloth as the item.

Selvage: The woven edges of a piece of cloth.

Sham: A pillow cover that can be easily removed by means of an overlapping back. These may be closed by buttons or ribbonlike ties.

Shantung: A form of slubbed silk, usually unbleached, made from pongee and occasionally woven with cotton as well as silk.

Shears: Scissors with large blades used for cutting fabric.

Silk: The only natural fiber that comes in filament form, it is made from the cocoon of the silkworm.

Slub: A thick, uneven section in a fiber that creates texture in the weave.

Soutache: A narrow braid, originally used on military uniforms, usually topstitched on in a central groove.

Strié: A fine, uneven vertical stripe.

Sugar bag: As with flour sacks, sugar bags were washed and bleached and the fabric recycled into drying towels and clothing by those who lived in rural areas of America in the 1920s and 1930s.

Swag: Looping folds of fabric used in draping curtains. The *jabot* is the part that hangs vertically.

Tabby: The simplest over-and-under fabric weave, such as children use to make pot holders. Also called a *plain weave*.

Taffeta: A plain weave made by using warp and filling yarns of equal weight, producing a firm, close weave. We tend to think of taffeta as a crisp, silk-like fabric, but it is really a weave. Cotton taffeta is a very useful decorative fabric.

Terry cloth: Also known as *Turkish toweling,* this cloth has uncut loops on front and back, or just on the front. Terry may be bleached, piece dyed, yarn dyed, printed, dobby woven, patterned on a Jacquard loom, or reversible. It is especially useful in bathrooms for towels, slipper-chair covers, pillows, and robes, or for beach towels.

Ticking: A tightly woven, compact striped cloth with a white background used for covering mattresses and pillows, and also, depending on the fashion, for upholstery.

Tie silk: A firm, pliable, resilient silk used for neckties, dressing gowns, and accessories.

Toile: A monotone print with an intricate, engraved quality, often of a historical, pictorial subject. The name is short for toile de Jouy; Jouy is a town in France where many famous toiles were printed. *Toile* is also used as a term for the muslin used to mock up a design for a garment or curtain.

Topstitch: A machine stitch that shows on the outside of a finished project.

Tufted fabric: Fabric into which fluffy twists of multiple cotton yarns are inserted or loom woven. Candlewick and chenille are examples of tufted fabrics. They are used for bedspreads, bath mats, and robes.

Tufting: A method of upholstering using thread, buttons, or decorative knots to hold fabric covering deep padding in place.

Turk's head: A globe-shaped, decorative handmade knot formed from cord or fabric tubing. Used as a self-fabric button.

Turkish corners: *See* French corners.

Turkish toweling: *See* Terry cloth.

Tussah: Named after the larvae of the silkworm, it is a rough ecru or brown silk with slubs made by uncultivated silkworms. Sometimes called wild silk, it is often used to make shantung and pongee.

Twill: A diagonal, stepped weave.

Under-curtains: Unlined curtains of a sheer fabric used in conjunction with heavier, more decorative curtains to preserve privacy but let in light.

Valance: *See* Pelmet.

Vinyl: A material with a chemically produced waterproof surface and a flexible fabric back. Can be found in colors and printed, as well as clear. Useful for covering outdoor items like chairs in beach houses and garden kneeling pads. When transparent, it is useful as a lining for shower curtains.

Voile: A thin, almost transparent fabric made of high-twist combed cotton or cotton blend.

Waffle weave, waffle cloth: Similar to honeycomb (a raised effect like the cellular comb of the honeybee) weave. When made in cotton, it is called waffle piqué.

Wale: The ribs or cords in corduroy or piqué fabrics.

Warp: The threads that run down a fabric. These threads are the first set up on a loom, then the weft or filling threads are woven in.

Warp-printing: A method of printing fabric in which a pattern is first printed, painted, or dyed on the warp, and then a plain filler is woven in, producing a softened effect.

Washable: A term referring to fabrics that will not shrink or fade when laundered, but not to be confused with wash-and-wear, which refers to items that can be washed by hand or in a washing machine at the warm-water setting and drip-dried to shed most wrinkles.

Wax print: A fabric produced by applying wax in a pattern onto cloth, dipping the cloth into dye, and then removing the wax, leaving the original uncolored cloth beneath. (*See also* Batik, Resist print.)

Weft: The threads that weave across the warp of a piece of fabric from selvage to selvage; sometimes called the *filling* or the *woof*.

Welt: Fabric cut in bias strips, filled with cording, and then stitched between seams to give contrast or emphasis to slipcovers or upholstery. Also known as *piping*. "Self welt" is used to indicate when the fabric for the item and the welt match. Double-welting is a less expensive way to trim upholstered furniture because the nail heads used to attach it can be hidden between the welts; single welts must be sewn on. Welting can also be gathered.

White goods: A term referring to goods bleached and finished in a white condition, such as batiste, cambric, dimity, lawn, muslin, organdy, piqué, sheeting, voile, and washable silk.

White on white: Usually refers to men's broadcloth or poplin shirting made on a dobby or Jacquard loom so that white motifs appear on a white ground. Can also be any cloth with a similar effect.

Windowpane check: A fabric pattern that outlines the check formation, leaving spaces within the checks similar to a drawing of windowpanes.

Woof: *See* Weft.

Wool: Fabric made from the clipped fur of sheep. There are many breeds, grades, and types of wool.

Worsted: Fabrics made from twisted wool yarns, including barathea, gabardine, and serge.

Yarn-dyed fabric: Fabric made from yarns dyed before they are made into cloth. Yarn-dyed fabrics are superior to piece-dyed fabrics because the threads are completely and individually covered in dye. (However, the dusty, casual look of piece-dyed cloth is sometimes more desirable from a fashion point of view.)

Zipper foot: A sewing machine attachment that enables the needle to stitch close to a raised object such as a zipper or welt. Some zipper feet can be adjusted to stitch to the right or to the left.

SOURCES

Here is a list of gleaned-along-the-way sources that might be of use to those who care about household linens. I have not included major department stores unless they carry specialized linens, nor are fabric companies "to the trade only" included.

It is difficult to keep up with the many companies that open and close, but this list is current as of our press date.

Household Linen, Fabric, and Related Items

ABC Carpet & Home
880 Broadway
New York, NY 10003
(212) 430-3000
Huge emporium on several floors and buildings supplying decorative items for the household, including large selection of household linens, decorative fabrics, and trimmings by the yard.

Ad Hoc Softwares
410 West Broadway
New York, NY 10013
(212) 925-2652
"A little linen closet in SoHo," plus china, clocks, scarves, wastepaper baskets, toys, vases, sleepware, and dog bowls.

Anichini Gallery
745 Fifth Avenue
New York, NY 10022
(212) 752-2130
Chenille, tapestry, neoclassic looks. American and imported Italian linens.

Jeffrey Aronoff
(212) 645-3155
Luxurious and handsome hand-woven chenille throws, coverlets, and scarves. By appointment only.

Ballard Design
1670 Defoor Avenue, NW
Atlanta, GA 30318-7528
(800) 367-2775
Catalog with many household items, including bed linens, table skirts, throws, closets, and shelves.

Banana Republic
Call (516) 873-0452
for store nearest you.
Cable blankets and other rugged linens.

Barney's
660 Madison Avenue
New York, NY 10022
(212) 826-8900
Selection of luxurious and imaginative bed, bath, and table linens, many imported from Italy.

Eddie Bauer
Call (800) 645-7467
for store nearest you.
Rugged blankets, throws, and other linens.

Bed & Bath & Beyond
620 Avenue of the Americas
(18th Street)
New York, NY 10011
(212) 255-3550
Or call for the store nearest you.

E. Braun & Co.
717 Madison Avenue
New York, NY 10021-8090
(212) 838-0650
(800) 372-7286
fax (212) 832-5640
Superior, generously cut sheets and

fine-quality towels coveted world-wide. Fine household and personal linens, mostly from Europe — Italy, France, Switzerland, and Germany — such as Cocoon silk products, with throws and quilts filled with silk floss. Catalog available. Custom-tailored bed linens and a wide selection of monograms worked on hand-guided machines.

Chambers
Mail-Order Department
P.O. Box 7841
San Francisco, CA
94112-7841
(800) 334-9790
Furnishings for the bed and bath and related accessories.

The Company Store
500 Company Store Road
La Crosse, WI 54601
(800) 285-3696
Bed linens, blankets, comforters, and bath towels.

Crate & Barrel
P.O. Box 9059
Wheeling, IL 60090-9059
(800) 323-5461
Kitchen, bed, and bath linens. Call for store near you.

Cuddledown of Maine
312 Canco Road
Portland, Maine 04103
(800) 323-6793
Comforters, bed and bath linens, nightwear, slippers, and furnishings.

Descamps
723 Madison Avenue
New York, NY 10022
(212) 355-2522
Superior quality bed and bath linens.

Di Sciascio Virginia
236 East 78th Street (between 2nd and 3rd Avenues)
New York, NY 10021
(212) 794-8807
Beautiful and unique selection of antique lace and vintage household linens.

Down & Quilt Shop
1225 Madison Avenue
(between 88th and 89th Streets)
New York, NY 10021
(212) 423-9358
518 Columbus Avenue
(at 85th Street)
New York, NY 10024
(212) 496-8980

Eldridge Textile Company
277 Grand Street
New York, NY 10013
(212) 925-1523
Bedroom and bath ensembles, kitchen accessories, window treatments.

Faces of Time
32 West 40th Street
New York, NY 10018
(212) 921-0822
A melange of vintage items, including household linens, candlesticks, suitcases, watches, sports equipment, and accessories for dressing tables and desks.

F & F Importers —
40th Street Decorators
265 West 40th Street
(between 7th and 8th Avenues)
(1 flight up)
New York, NY 10018
(212) 354-5166
(212) 840-7444
French tergal curtains, bedspreads, tablecloths, ready-made and custom-made draperies, venetian vertical blinds and shades, wallpapers, and cotton prints.

Fanny Doolittle
Corner of Routes 311 and 22
Patterson, NY 12563
Vintage jewelry, furniture, and objects, with a selection of white-on-white household linens.

Felissimo
10 West 56th Street
New York, NY 10019
(212) 247-5656
A unique selection of household and decorative items, including some unusual domestic linens in a multilevel specialty store.

Fine Linens by Oswald
1193 Lexington Avenue
(at 81st Street)
New York, NY 10028
(212) 737-0520

Laura Fisher
1050 2nd Avenue
(between 55th and 56th Streets)
Gallery #84
New York, NY 10022
(212) 838-2596 or by appointment (212) 866-6033
Large, fine selection of antique and

traditional quilts, including Amish quilts, hooked rugs, paisleys, coverlets, Indian blankets, home furnishings, American folk art, and more.

Forster David & Co.
750 Madison Avenue
(near 65th Street)
New York, NY 10022
(212) 861-8989
Corporate/institutional sales division, now part of Léron, supplying high-end hospitality business, such as banqueting tablecloths for hotels, linens for country clubs, and more.

Frette Inc.
799 Madison Avenue
New York, NY 10021
(212) 988-5221/2
and at Bergdorf Goodman:
2 West 58th Street
New York, NY 10019
and at:
449 North Rodeo Drive
Los Angeles, CA
(310) 273-8540
New York office:
200 West 57th Street, Suite 1105
New York, NY 10019
(212) 262-6740
Home office:
Via Visconti di Modrone
15-20122 Milano, Italy
02/77709.1
Many other locations in Italy and in cities all over the world.
Fine, luxurious household linens made in Italy by the same family-owned company for over a hundred years.

Frontgate
2800 Henkle Drive
Lebanon, OH 45036-8894
(800) 626-6488
A catalog with many household items, including bath linens, shelves, and armoires.

Garnet Hill
Box 262 Main Street
Franconia, NH 03589-0262
(800) 622-6216
Specializes in high-quality bed linens, pillows, curtains, furniture, and clothing made of natural fibers.

The Gazebo
114 East 57th Street
New York, NY 10022
(212) 832-7077
(800) 998-7077
Quilts, appliquéd and pieced curtains, braided rugs, rag rugs, handmade toys, tree decorations, and other handcrafted treasures. Catalog available.

Gracious Home
1217 Third Avenue
(at 70th Street)
New York, NY 10021
(212) 988-8990
Huge emporium supplying most needs for the household, including sheets, pillowcases, comforters, towels, linens, fabric, and wallpaper.

Jean Hoffman Antiques
207 East 66th Street
New York, NY 10021
(212) 535-6930
(212) 249-0866
Antique bed and table linens and

laces, pillows, lace panels, and lace curtains.

Hold Everything
P.O. Box 7807
San Francisco, CA 94120-7807
(800) 421-2264
fax (800) 421-5153
Big range of all kinds of closet and storage units. Stores across the country.

Ikea
Call (212) 308-4532
for store nearest you.
A wide variety of good, inexpensive housewares.

Jo Productions
594 Broadway, Suite 904
(near Houston Street)
New York, NY 10002
(212) 965-0240
Custom-made reversible quilts, including large velvet quilts ($100–$300). By appointment only.

Kensington Collection
Good Catalogue Company
545 SE International Way
Portland, OR 97222
(800) 225-3870
Among household, garden, and decorative items in this catalog are table and bed linens and coverlets.

Kitchen & Home
P.O. Box 2527
Lacrosse, WI 54602-2527
(800) 414-5544
fax (800) 238-0271
Includes some table and kitchen linens.

Calvin Klein

645 Madison Avenue
New York, NY 10022
(212) 292-9000

As well as being featured in this listed store, Calvin Klein household products are sold in some department stores and can be seen in various catalogs. Calvin Klein has recently added bed linens for infants — crib sheets, blankets, and comforters, designed in the firm's chic minimalist style.

Ralph Lauren

867 Madison Avenue
New York, NY 10021
(212) 606-2100
Ralph Lauren Home:
1185 Avenue of the Americas
New York, NY 10036
(212) 642-8700

As well as being available in this listed store, Ralph Lauren household linens are sold in some department stores and are featured in various catalogs.

Laytner's Linen

2270 Broadway
New York, NY 10024
(212) 724-1080
237 East 86th Street
New York, NY 10028
(212) 996-4439

Sheets, blankets, throws, comforters, towels, shower curtains, bath accessories, table linens, rugs, and pillows.

Leron Inc.

750 Madison Avenue
(at 65th Street)
New York, NY 10021
(212) 753-6700

Custom-embroidered handkerchiefs, fine lingerie and trousseau items, robes, golf pants, crib sets, point de Beauvais embroidery, Italian Fuselli lace, place mats, and table, bath, and bed linens; less expensive bed and table linens under the name Tambourine.

Liberty Fabrics

295 Fifth Avenue
New York, NY 10003
(212) 684-3100

Many different fabrics, including those with a distinctive tiny floral look.

Linen & Lace

4 Lafayette Street
Washington, MO 63090-2541
(800) 332-5223
fax (314) 239-0070

Exquisite Scottish lace, Egyptian and European cotton on Nottingham lace looms, archival lace, wedding handkerchiefs, drawn-thread work, and fine lace curtains. Catalog available.

Françoise Nunnallé

(212) 246-4281

A wonderful collection of antique bed and table linens of museum quality; also textile pillows made from antique fabric from the fifteenth century on; nineteenth-century curtain tiebacks, 1760–1820 Sheffield plates, and antique soup tureens. By appointment only.

The Ohio Hempery

P.O. Box 18
Guysville, OH 45735
(800) BUY-HEMP
fax (614) 662 6446
e-mail: hempery@hempery.com
website: www.hempery.com

Clothing, fabric, products, books, all made of or related to hemp. Catalog available.

Orvis

Historic Route 7A
Manchester, VT 05254-0798
(800) 541-3541

Rugged blankets and throws. Catalog available.

Paron Fabrics

56 West 57th Street
New York, NY 10019
(212) 247-6451
Paron East:
855 Lexington Avenue
(at 64th Street)
New York, NY 10021
(212) 772-7353
Paron West Corp.:
206 West 40th Street
New York, NY 10018
(212) 768-3266

Source for *better* discount fabrics.

Susan Parrish Antiques

390 Bleeker Street
(near 10th Street)
New York, NY 10011
(212) 645-5020

A good collection of patchwork quilts.

Past Times
280 Summer Street
Boston, MA 02210-1182
(800) 621-6020
A catalog originating in England that has many household items, including unusual table linens, towels, lap rugs, and throws.

Pénélope
19 Avenue Victor Hugo
Paris, France
(011) 33-1-45-00-90-90
Exquisitely embroidered napkins, tablecloths, and place mats, made by a group of homebound artisans for a nonprofit organization in return for a salary and social support. Used in many French embassies around the world. Tablecloth and four napkins start at $400, run to $1,200 for a twelve-napkin set.

Pierre Deux Fabrics
870 Madison Avenue
New York, NY 10021
(212) 570-9343
Fabrics and household accessories with a distinctively French Provençal look.

D. Porthault & Co.
18 East 69th Street
New York, NY 10021
(212) 688-1661
Fine and famous selection of household linens, with distinctive

An exemplary collection of white-on-white antique linens from Françoise Nunnallé in New York City. (Photo by Jim Chervenak.)

prints and hand-hemmed scalloped edges. (See Monograms as well).

Pottery Barn
P.O. Box 7044
San Francisco, CA 94120-7044
(800) 922-5507
Bed linens, pillows, furniture, and accessories. Call for store near you.

Pratesi Linens
829 Madison Avenue
New York, NY 10021
(212) 288-2315
Fine household linens made by hundred-year-old family business near Florence, Italy. Specialize in fabrics such as Angelskin, damask, lace, linen, cashmere blankets and robes, terry, tablecloths, and new division of baby linen items.

Real Goods
555 Leslie Street
Ukiah, CA 95482-5576
(800) 762-7325
Organic cotton and hemp bed linen.

Rue de France
78 Thames Street
Newport, RI 02840
(800) 777-0998
fax (401) 846-6821
"The Catalogue of French Country Living." Sells exclusive lace fabric by the yard, matching lace trim, and includes sewing instructions. Also sells Pierre Deux fabrics.

Savannah
156 Sullivan Street
New York, NY 10014
(212) 673-2693

Small shop with antique household items and good selection of vintage linens — napkins, towels, sheets, pillow shams, and tablecloths.

Z. Schweitzer Linens
475 Columbus Avenue
(between 81st and 82nd Streets)
New York, NY 10024
(212) 799-9629
1132 Madison Avenue
(between 84th and 85th Streets)
New York, NY 10028
(212) 249-8361
1053 Lexington Avenue
(between 74th and 75th Streets)
New York, NY 10021
(212) 570-0236
Large selection of many brands of fine household linens, at reasonable prices, in three New York stores. Catalog available.

Jillann Stewart Textiles
Unit 19 Govan Workspace
6 Harmony Row
Glasgow, G51 3BA U.K.
(011) 44 (0)141-445-5554
Soft furnishings, pillows, lap throws, made using a photo process and mixed luxurious fabrics.

Sur la Table
1765 Sixth Avenue South
Seattle, WA 98134-1608
Amid mostly table and kitchen equipment can be found table mats, runners, and napkins.

Williamsburg
The Colonial Williamsburg Foundation
Colonial Williamsburg
P.O. Box 3532
Williamsburg, VA 23187-3532
(800) 446-9240

A catalog of furnishings, textiles, and accessories that include bed linens based on fabrics in the museum.

Williams-Sonoma
P.O. Box 7456
San Francisco, CA 94120-7456
(800) 541-2233
Kitchen and table linens as well as items for cooks. Call for store near you.

Wolfman Gold & Good Co.
116 Greene Street
New York, NY
(212) 431-1888
Kitchen, bed, and bath linen.

Zimman's Fabrics
80 Market Street
Lynn, MA 01901
(617) 598-9432
A good selection of fabrics by the yard.

Trimmings

Hyman Hendler & Sons
67 West 38th Street
New York, NY 10018
(212) 840-8393
fax (212) 704-4237
The finest in ribbons and velvets.

Madame Frou Frou
231 West 40th Street
New York, NY 10018
(212) 840-0682
Fancy trimmings, including fringes, tassels, and braids.

M & J Trimming
    1008 Sixth Avenue (between
37th and 38th Streets)
New York, NY 10018
(212) 391-9072
fax (212) 764-5854
Big selection of trimming, including
lace, braid, rope, and more.

So-Good, Inc.
    28 West 38th Street
New York, NY 10018
(212) 398-0236
Novelty ribbons and trimmings.

Tinsel Trading Co.
    47 West 38th Street
New York NY 10018
(212) 730-1030
Large selection of unusual trimmings.

Monograms

Most of the fine household linen
specialty stores not only provide a
monogramming service but can also
produce embroidery on their linens
keyed to a special design element in
your rooms, such as a detail from a
wallpaper or fabric. Charges vary
according to the design.

Monograms were traditionally
used on household linens in order
to distinguish one's own linens
when they were washed at river-
banks. Now more than ever, people
carry on the custom, though the
need is no longer the same.

Most catalogs that sell household linens supply a small range of
simple monograms for an extra
charge.

*This monogrammed towel was
designed by the firm of Wagner Van
Dam Designs & Decoration, New
York, for the 1997 Kips Bay show-
house. It was embroidered by Penn &
Fletcher, Inc.*

Penn & Fletcher
    242 West 30th Street
New York, NY 10036
(212) 239-6868
Embroidery on linens and monograms made to order.

**Pfaff Sewing Center of
Manhattan**
    1077 Third Avenue
New York, NY 10021
(212) 755-8811
Or contact:
Pfaff American Sales Corp.
610 Winters Avenue
Paramus, NJ 07653
The latest computerized sewing
machines have monogram capa-

bility. At Pfaff, for instance, there
are six alphabet styles available,
plus other motifs, and the fabric to
be worked has to be held in a
special hoop.

D. Porthault & Co.
    18 East 69th Street
New York, NY 10021
(212) 688-1660
French monogram designer Sylvie
Levrai (trained at L'école des arts
decoratifs) designs unique monograms by painting on transparent
acetate so that the client can see
how it will look on fabric. Porthault
has more than 2,000 designs in
their archives to inspire and work
from. (See the bibliography for
Porthault's new book on monograms.)

Cleaning

**The Textile Conservation
Laboratory**
    At the Cathedral of St. John the
Divine (Camille Breeze)
1047 Amsterdam Avenue
(at 112th Street)
New York, NY 10025
(212) 316-7523
Cleans and conserves good quality
rugs and fabric, including antique
quilts, and stores them in acid-free
boxes.

SELECTED *Bibliography*

Beeton, Isabella. *Mrs. Beeton's Book of Household Management.* London: Ward, Lock & Co., 1909.

Burnham, Dorothy K. *Warp and Weft: A Textile Terminology.* Toronto: Hunter Rose Company, Royal Ontario Museum, 1980.

Calloway, Stephen. *Twentieth-Century Decoration: The Domestic Interior from 1900 to the Present Day.* London: Weidenfeld & Nicholson, 1988.

De Bonneville, Françoise, with an introduction by Marc Porthault. *The Book of Fine Linen.* Paris: Flammarion, 1994.

A Dictionary of Textile Terms. Danville, Virginia: Dan River, 1971.

Lebeau, Caroline. *Fabrics: The Decorative Art of Textiles.* New York: Clarkson Potter, 1994.

Levey, Santine M. *Lace: A History.* London: W. S. Maney & Son Limited, Victoria and Albert publication, 1983.

Montgomery, Florence M. *Textiles in America, 1650–1870.* New York: W. W. Norton, 1984.

Niles, Bo. *White by Design.* New York: Stewart, Tabori & Chang, 1984.

Nylander, Jane C. *Fabrics for Historic Buildings.* Rev. ed. Washington, D.C.: Preservation Press, National Trust for Historic Preservation, 1990.

Peterson, Harold L. *Americans at Home.* New York: Charles Scribner's Sons, 1971.

Praz, Mario. *Interior Decoration: An Illustrated History from Pompeii to Art Nouveau.* New York:

Thames and Hudson, 1982.

Salvy, Eglé. *Chiffrer le Linge de Maison: Créations D. Porthault.* Berkeley, CA: Locis Publications, 1996.

Sandwith, Hermione and Sheila Stainton. *The National Trust Manual of Housekeeping.* London: Viking, 1964.

Scofield, Elizabeth and Peggy Zalamea. *20th Century Linens and Lace: A Guide to Identification, Care and Prices of Household Linens.* Atglen, PA: Schiffer Publishing, 1995.

Talbot, Constance. *The Complete Book of Sewing: Dressmaking and Sewing for the Home Made Easy.* New York: International Readers League, 1943.

Thornton, Peter. *Authentic Decor: The Domestic Interior, 1620–1920.* London: Weidenfeld & Nicholson, 1984.

Wingate, Dr. Isobel B. *Fairchild's Dictionary of Textiles.* 6th ed. New York: Fairchild Publications, 1979.

Wright, J. and D. Hambleton. *All Things Wise and Wonderful.* Pasadena: Pasadena Art Alliance, 1975.

DESIGNED BY SUSAN MARSH

TYPESET IN FAIRFIELD, BAUER BODONI, AND SNELL ROUNDHAND

PRINTED BY TIEN WAH PRESS, SINGAPORE